JUN — 1999

RAÚL JULIÁ

Actor and Humanitarian

Bárbara C. Cruz

Enslow Publishers, Inc.

44 Fadem Road	PO Box 38
Box 699	Aldershot
Springfield, NJ 07081	Hants GU12 6BP
USA	UK

Para mis padres Elsa e Ignacio Acosta, mis primeros maestros sobre América Latina

Library of Congress Cataloging-in-Publication Data

Cruz, Bárbara.
    Raul Julia: actor and humanitarian / Bárbara C. Cruz
       p. cm. — (Hispanic biographies)
    Includes bibliographical references and index.
    Summary: Relates the life and career of the Puerto Rican native who came to the United States where he became an outstanding actor and a prominent humanitarian until his recent death.
    ISBN 0-7660-1040-6
    1. Julia, Raul—Juvenile literature. 2. Actors—Puerto Rico—Biography—Juvenile literature. 3. Hispanic American actors—Biography—Juvenile literature. [1. Julia, Raul. 2. Hispanic American actors. 3. Actors and actresses. 4. Hispanic Americans—Biography.]
I. Title. II. Series.
PN2434.J86C78   1998
792'.028'092—dc21
[B]
                                  97-37827
                                        CIP
                                        AC

Printed in the United States of America

10 9 8 7 6 5 4 3 2 1

Illustration Credits: Ron Rinaldi, p. 6; Billy Rose Theatre Collection, The New York Library for the Performing Arts; Astor, Lenox, and Tilden Foundations, pp. 11, 37, 39; Bárbara C. Cruz, pp. 15, 25, 44; Created by Enslow Publishers, Inc., p. 17; Courtesy Juliá family, pp. 19, 22, 65, 87; The Puerto Rican Traveling Theatre Company, Inc., p. 34; José Rosario, pp. 49, 56; The Hunger Project, ©1987, p. 53; Paulist Productions, Pacific Palisades, California, p. 69; Kamala Lopez-Dawson, pp. 78, 80, 84; Freedom House Photos, New York, p. 97; Ronald Martinez, p. 101.

Cover Illustration: Ron Rinaldi

CONTENTS

ACKNOWLEDGMENTS

I would like to acknowledge the efforts and support of the following individuals who were instrumental in bringing this project to fruition:

Susan Wright and Merel Poloway Juliá, who provided valuable information and cherished family photographs;

Leonard R. Sussman, executive director of Freedom House, for furnishing priceless photos of Juliá in El Salvador;

Kamala López-Dawson, actress, screenwriter, and film producer, who graciously gave of her time and contributed photos from her personal archive;

Lilian Hurst, who shared her memories and her extensive clippings;

Jennifer Groendal and Robert Driver, without whose help I could not have done such extensive research;

Jack and Jean Vine, for their helpful reviews and warm support throughout;

Kevin A. Yelvington, who is more of an inspiration to me than he knows.

Raúl Juliá

CHAPTER ONE

ON THE ROAD TO STARDOM

Raúl Juliá came to New York City from his native Puerto Rico to pursue his dream of being an actor. By 1971, he had been in the United States only seven years. With a height of over six feet, a vibrant voice, and hooded gray eyes, he had a powerful stage presence. Broadway theater directors and Hollywood film producers were already taking note of the young Puerto Rican actor. To the majority of Americans, however, he was unknown.

Then, one day, Juliá got a call from his agent that would bring his smiling face into millions of American homes every morning. The children's television program *Sesame Street* wanted Juliá to become a part of the regular cast. The show's producers felt that they needed to make an effort in reaching the children of the *barrios* (Spanish-speaking neighborhoods). Up until this point, there had been no educational programs on television that consistently featured Hispanic characters. When Latino children turned on their television sets, they rarely saw anyone who looked like them. Juliá acknowledged his selection by saying, "It's true that I am in *Sesame Street* because I am Puerto Rican. I tape two or three times a week, and all of my segments are in Spanish."[1]

Cis Corman, who was responsible for casting the actors on *Sesame Street*, was impressed by Juliá. She immediately recognized his stage presence and his genuine desire to be on the program. Corman also realized that Juliá cared about kids, especially those with minority backgrounds.[2] Soon after his audition, Juliá learned that he had been hired.

Sesame Street had been on the air less than a year when Juliá was chosen to play Rafael the Fixit Man. Along with Luis, played by Emilio Delgado (who can still be seen on the show), Rafael operated a repair shop.

While he was on *Sesame Street*, membership in Juliá's fan club grew among four- and five-year-olds. At the time, Juliá said: "As soon as I go out of the house in the morning, some tot comes up to me and says, 'Hi, Rafaelo!'"[3] But Juliá did not mind. In fact, he made it a point to stop and sign autographs if he was asked.

While he was appearing on *Sesame Street*, Juliá was given an important opportunity. The Broadway theater producer and director Joe Papp asked him to appear in the role of Proteus in a musical version of Shakespeare's romantic comedy *Two Gentlemen of Verona*. Ever since he was a boy in Puerto Rico, Juliá had loved Shakespeare. He was delighted with the offer. The role of Proteus was too good to refuse.

In *Two Gentlemen of Verona*, Juliá played the part of a charming but foolish and unfaithful young man who gets involved in two different love triangles. On opening night Juliá was very nervous. Even though he had done the deep-breathing exercises that he had learned in yoga class, he was still scared.[4] After that first performance, the cast gathered at Tavern on the Green, a restaurant in the middle of Central Park. There they celebrated their accomplishment and awaited the first theater reviews. The critics not only applauded the play, but also highly praised Juliá in particular.[5]

So, during the day, Juliá worked on *Sesame Street*. Then, at night, he performed in *Two Gentlemen of Verona*. It was a strenuous schedule. *Sesame Street*'s Emilio Delgado also happened to be Juliá's understudy in *Two Gentlemen of Verona*. The friend and actor remembers how sometimes Juliá, overcome with exhaustion, would fall asleep in the makeup chair. "But," says Delgado, "he always put his all into everything he did. He gave 100 percent."[6] Despite his fatigue and the hectic work schedule, Juliá never missed a show.

Theater critics and the public loved *Two Gentlemen of Verona*. The success prompted Papp to extend the play's run and move it to a permanent location on Broadway. For his superb performance in the musical, Juliá received a Tony Award nomination for Best Actor. The Tony Awards are given every year to recognize the people who did the best job in theater. Juliá was delighted with the nomination, which he felt was a big turning point for him.[7]

As if he were not busy enough, the following summer, while he was still performing in *Two Gentlemen of Verona* at the St. James Theater, he also accepted a part in a production of *Hamlet* at the outdoor Delacorte Theater in Central Park. In this dark Shakespearean tragedy, a Danish prince is tormented by the ghost of his father. The play's most famous scene is when the prince contemplates whether to commit suicide. Papp cast the play with well-known actors such as Stacy Keach, James Earl Jones, and Colleen Dewhurst. Juliá was cast in the role of Osric. One reviewer wrote that it was one of the finest casts

Critics praised Raúl Juliá's work as Osric in a production of *Hamlet* at the outdoor Delacorte Theater in New York City's Central Park.

ever assembled for the play and should "be regarded as one of the great *Hamlet*s of our time."[8]

Because Osric does not appear until the final act, Juliá would take his bows after finishing *Two Gentlemen of Verona*, be whisked away by limousine to the Delacorte, change quickly into costume, and appear as Osric at the end of the play. It was a difficult feat not only because of the physical exhaustion, but also because the roles were so different. For even the most veteran and talented performer, simultaneously appearing in two such dissimilar plays would be an extraordinary accomplishment. Still, critics praised Juliá's Osric. One theater reviewer wrote, "I have never in my life seen such a coolly stylish Osric. . . . It never occurred to me that Osric could have so much grace, passion, and venom."[9] Critics also marveled that such a fine actor could be so humble—that he could play a leading role in one play and a bit part in another. It was becoming apparent to all that Juliá was very gifted.

Whether he was playing a familiar Latino character in a children's show, a British gentleman in a musical, or a Danish court attendant in a Shakespearean tragedy, Raúl Juliá's talent as a versatile and capable actor was becoming well known. He was definitely on the road to stardom.

MI VIEJO
SAN JUAN

Raúl Rafael Carlos Juliá y Arcelay was born on March 9, 1940, in San Juan, Puerto Rico. He was the eldest of Raúl Juliá and Olga Arcelay's four children. The family lived comfortably in a thriving neighborhood in San Juan.

Raúl's family was Roman Catholic, like the majority of Puerto Ricans. Catholicism was introduced in Puerto Rico in the fifteenth century by the Spanish. Christopher Columbus landed there in 1493, and the Spanish settled a colony in 1509, in part to mine the gold that had been found on an earlier visit. The name given to the island means "rich port" in Spanish. The explorer Juan Ponce de León officially founded the city of San Juan in 1521. The gold mines were soon exhausted, however, and the colony's economy became centered on the cultivation and processing of sugarcane. The island was officially named La Isla de San Juan Bautista de Puerto Rico.

At first, the Europeans forced the peaceful Taino people that had been living there to work in the mines and cane fields. The hard work, terrible conditions, and diseases brought by the Europeans eventually killed the American Indian population. To satisfy Europe's growing appetite for sugar, enslaved Africans were brought to work on the plantations. Until the late 1800s, slavery dominated Puerto Rico's history.

In 1898, the United States entered into a war with Spain, which owned the island. As a victor in the war, the United States gained control of Puerto Rico, Guam, and the Philippine Islands. In 1900, Congress officially made Puerto Rico a United States unincorporated territory, which enabled the United States to exercise a great amount of control over the island. In 1952, Puerto Rico became a commonwealth, which gave the island more control over local affairs. Puerto Ricans on the island are U.S. citizens but are not allowed to vote for the president, have no representation in Congress, and do not pay U.S. taxes.

Old San Juan, where Raúl Juliá was born in 1940, retains much of its colonial charm.

Puerto Rico is one of the islands, along with Cuba, Jamaica, and Hispaniola, that makes up the Greater Antilles in the Caribbean. Much of Puerto Rico is mountainous, and it is relatively small—just one hundred miles long and thirty-five miles wide. San Juan is the capital and commercial center of the island. Although Puerto Ricans identify themselves primarily as Latinos and speak mostly Spanish, the influence from the United States is significant, and most Puerto Ricans speak English as well. By law, schools in Puerto Rico are required to teach English a minimum of seventy minutes each day.[1]

Raúl's father, whose name was also Raúl, claimed to have brought pizza to the island. As a young man he had traveled to the United States and studied to become an electrical engineer at Tri State University in Angola, Indiana. When he returned to San Juan, he worked for a while as an engineer but soon opened a gas station and body shop. Eventually, however, he turned it into a restaurant called La Cueva del Chicken Inn. *Cueva* means "cave" in Spanish, and the restaurant was decorated to look like the inside of a Spanish gypsy cave. The restaurant is also credited for introducing chicken-in-a-basket to Puerto Rico. But it was the pizza that Juliá enjoyed most, calling it "the best in the world."[2]

Raúl's mother, Olga Arcelay, was an amateur singer who sang opera and participated in the choir at the

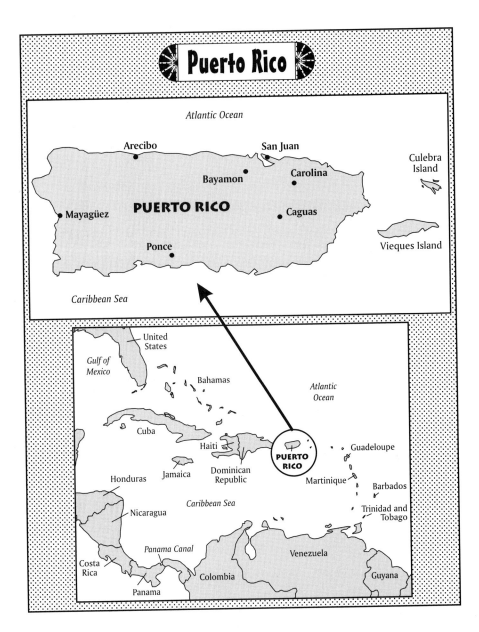

The mountainous island of Puerto Rico is relatively small—only one hundred miles long and thirty-five miles wide.

local Catholic church. Raúl's great-aunt, María González, was a zarzuela singer. Zarzuelas are Spanish operettas that were popular in Spain and Latin America. Later, when asked where he got his own theatrical interest, Raúl credited his great-aunt.[3] Unfortunately, in those times, it was not appropriate for a young woman to leave home and join the theater, so his great-aunt was never able to develop her talent.

Raúl had three younger siblings: his brother, Rafael, and two sisters, María Eugenia and Olga María. People remember the Juliá family as being "musical, very humorous, very dramatic."[4] Raúl remembers growing up "in an atmosphere where there was always music around."[5] He also remembers being encouraged to perform at parties "just for the heck of it."[6]

Raúl was considered a quiet, soft-spoken boy. When it was time to enroll little Raúl in school, the well-to-do family placed him in a private Catholic school with an excellent reputation. The school was run by North American nuns who spoke little or no Spanish.

Raúl's introduction to the theater came early. When Raúl was just five years old and in the first grade, he was cast as the devil in a school play. To get him ready for the part, his great-aunt María made his costume: velvet, with sparkling sequins, and a little pair of horns for his head. He rehearsed his part daily, anticipating the big event. On the day of the play, when it was time for his part, the usually shy Raúl jumped on stage,

Young Raúl (center), pictured here with his mother, Olga, father, Raúl Sr., and brother, Rafael, had a happy childhood in his theatrically inclined family.

threw himself on the floor, and let out a blood-curdling screech: "Oooooooeeeeeooooo!"[7] "It was a marvelous experience," Raúl later said. "I entered and let go of myself. I became sort of like possessed or something."[8] Raúl's parents and teachers were alarmed, thinking that the boy was having some sort of fit. At that point he calmly stood up and started saying his lines. After that, he was in every school play.[9]

That event gave Raúl his first clue that acting was what he wanted to do. He remembered, "It was like jumping into an abyss [a deep hole] . . . taking the chance. You know when you dive for the first time from the high board? It was that kind of feeling, very exciting! The whole audience was taken aback at the transformation in this young kid."[10] That first theatrical experience was also important for Raúl in another way. He found that he had the talent to do something people enjoyed.[11] He also realized, "Being an actor has to do with being liked. I learned that as far back as the first grade, back in San Juan. Being acknowledged by an audience [means] that you've done something they like and enjoy."[12]

For fun, Raúl and his siblings sometimes went to the movies. Going to the movies was a popular pastime in Puerto Rico. The cool, dark theaters provided a welcome break from the heat outside. When Raúl saw Errol Flynn in *Robin Hood*, he was charmed. He later said, "It was one of the first movies I saw, and I decided that was the life for me."[13] He was also impressed by the British actor Laurence Olivier and by José Ferrer, a Puerto Rican actor who went on to gain international popularity.

Raúl's sense of theatrics led him to be somewhat of a prankster. One time, he sat at the family's piano, which was located next to a window, in full view of people passing by. He put on a classical music record out of sight from the window and pretended to play the piano. People walking by were astonished that such a young boy could play so wonderfully![14]

Raúl was also a very sensitive boy, and he was strongly impressed by his parents' humanitarian concerns. Both Raúl Sr. and Olga would take homeless children into their home.[15] Olga Arcelay was involved in a Catholic youth group that provided assistance to the needy. Her efforts were later recognized by the Catholic University of Puerto Rico in Ponce. Observing his parents' kindness and concern with the needy and hungry made an impact on the young boy—an impact that would have significant effects later in adulthood.

By the time Raúl was in the seventh grade, he had become fluent in English. From early on, Raúl loved the plays of William Shakespeare. Although many of Shakespeare's plays were difficult to understand at first, Juliá admired the poetic words, the rhythm of the verses, and the stories that seemed to be timeless and universal.

Raúl in his high school graduation photo

Raúl credits this passion to the Jesuit priests who were his high school teachers. For his secondary education, Raúl attended Colegio San Ignacio de Loyola. At his school, they would stage classroom productions of *Julius Caesar*, *Hamlet*, *The Tempest*, and *King Lear*. He was in every play the school produced. When Raúl graduated from San Ignacio de Loyola, he was in the school's second graduating class, which had only eight students.

To please his parents, Raúl then enrolled in college, at the Universidad de Puerto Rico. He began by studying psychology, then medicine, and finally settled on a career in law. "I only went to the university to make my parents happy," Raúl later explained. "I took all the [classes] I liked and knew I could pass without too much trouble."[16] He went from one department to another but was never satisfied with any of the academic programs.[17] As a hobby, he continued to act in locally produced plays and nightclub shows. He eventually earned a bachelor's degree in liberal arts from the Universidad de Puerto Rico.

Juliá soon realized that becoming a lawyer was not what he really wanted to do. "There came a time," he said, "when I really looked inside myself and said, 'What do you want to do? What do you *really* want to do?'" He realized then and there that what he really liked best was acting.[18] But he still doubted whether he could make a living at it. "As a child, I thought theater was a school thing," he reflected. "Something for people to come and see and laugh at. I never thought of it as a way of making a living. You know that thing all our parents tell us: 'You've got to work hard if you want to make a living.' Well, acting was just too much fun; it was never hard work."[19]

Raúl became more and more involved in the theater scene in San Juan. He appeared in the Shakespearean tragedy *Macbeth*. Because much of the story takes place in a Scottish castle, the play was performed in an ancient fort in Old San Juan. That section of the city is considered by many to be the most beautiful because of its narrow cobblestone streets and old-fashioned buildings. El Morro, the fort at the entrance of San Juan Harbor, was built more than three hundred years ago.

During this time, Raúl performed on the "Ted Mack Amateur Hour" and was part of a singing group called the Lamplighters. Despite his increasing involvement in San Juan's theatrical world, Raúl's parents continued to hope that he would come to his senses and take up a more stable career. Lilian Hurst, a Puerto Rican actress who now lives in the United States, recalls an incident with Raúl's mother:

> I saw Raúl for the first time in Puerto Rico, singing "La Bolita" ("The Little Ball"), a lively merengue tune. I remember that he was hilarious because he sang the song using many different

Raúl Juliá studied law, among other subjects, at the Universidad de Puerto Rico.

accents—Spanish, French, and German, just to name a few. During this time I had a television show and the producer asked me what I wanted for the following program. Immediately, I said "I want him [Juliá]!" So we called Juliá at his home and his mother answered the telephone. When she realized what we wanted, she replied: "No, I think you are mistaken. My son will not be an actor." Little did she know![20]

Soon Lilian and Raúl were both cast in a song-and-dance revue at the San Juan hotel El Convento. One evening, Raúl caught the eye of Orson Bean, who was vacationing on the island. Bean was a stage actor and comedian who later gained popularity appearing on game shows in the United States. Bean recalled: "He stood out so much, I spoke to him afterwards. I told him I thought he was incredibly talented."[21] Juliá told him that he had been thinking of going to Europe to study acting. Bean instead suggested that Juliá go to New York to develop his talent. He said to Juliá, "Why don't you come visit New York? I think New York would be very good for you."[22] He scribbled his telephone number on a piece of paper and urged the budding actor to consider his proposal.

After thinking it over, Raúl decided that his best chance at establishing a career in acting was to take Bean's advice. When he told his parents, they were horrified, but they agreed to support him.[23]

But then something happened that almost kept Raúl from leaving the island. Just as he was about to depart, his younger brother, Rafael, was killed in a car accident. Rafael was seventeen years old. His family was thrown into a state of shock, grieving over their loss. For Raúl, it was a very difficult time. He said:

> It was a great period of sorrow. It is something you never forget. You do your best not to carry it around as a burden or brick. You try to use it as a learning experience. But you feel a lot of guilt. You wonder, "Why him and not me?" At the same time, that kind of tragedy enables you to understand tragedy. Pain, sorrow, and guilt . . . all that stuff keeps coming up.[24]

After consulting with his family, Raúl decided to carry out his plans and go to New York. Although he loved his native Puerto Rico, he realized that, as an actor, it was necessary to leave the island in order to expand and develop his career. The opportunities in his homeland were simply too limited. He was twenty-four years old when he left Puerto Rico for the bright lights of the Big Apple.

THE BIG APPLE

When Raúl Juliá first arrived in New York in 1964 with nothing more than a suitcase full of clothes, the city had been blanketed by a terrible snowstorm. Coming from the mild tropical climate of Puerto Rico, Juliá was unprepared for the brutal cold. He had never even seen snow before. He was shivering, his nose started dripping, and it was not long before he started dreaming of his native island.[1]

At first, Juliá lived in a small, one-room, fifteen-dollar-a-week furnished apartment on the Upper West Side of Manhattan. He and his roommate, a fellow

Puerto Rican actor, had to scrape together pennies to make ends meet. Juliá recalled that they used to buy *rabadillas* (chicken backs), which cost only twenty-five cents for four. They would also get bread and grapes, both relatively inexpensive, and they would eat that once a day.[2] He admitted: "There were some hard times."[3]

To earn money, Juliá took a training course on how to sell pens. His job was to demonstrate the pens in department and grocery stores and sell as many as he could. The pens looked expensive but were cheaply made. His pitch was "Come and see! I will give you two pens for the price of one! Come and see!" When he realized that he was cheating the customers, he quit after only one day.[4]

Juliá then found work selling magazine subscriptions over the telephone. Starting off the day was always the most difficult part for him. He remembered, "The first call of the day was always the worst. I always thought, 'Oh, man, what poor person am I waking up at nine this morning?' I used to sit there with the phone book in front of me, looking up all the Spanish names. I figured if I talked Spanish, I'd have more rapport."[5] But that job did not last long either.

When he could, Juliá went to the theater. New York City offers more plays and musicals than any other place in the United States, so there were lots of shows from which to choose. When Lilian Hurst, Juliá's friend from Puerto Rico, visited him in New York, she invited him to the theater. He was delighted because it was a treat he could not usually afford.[6] When he attended his first Broadway show, he thought, "My God, you can actually make a living!"[7] In addition to the theaters on Broadway, there are many other, smaller theaters known as off-Broadway. Juliá immediately began answering open casting calls for shows both on and off Broadway.

To become better prepared for the casting calls, Juliá also took acting lessons from Wynn Handman, a drama coach who was the artistic director of the American Place Theater. Handman had been recommended to Juliá by Orson Bean, back when Bean had first met the young actor in San Juan. Handman later recalled how his acting studio immediately became a "more charming place" when Juliá started attending classes and how the young actor never missed a lesson.[8]

Within two months, Juliá won a part in an off-Broadway production of *La Vida Es Sueño* (Life Is a Dream), a play written by the seventeenth-century Spanish author Pedro Calderón de la Barca. The production was double-cast, that is, it had two full casts of actors. One set of actors performed the play in English and one set performed in Spanish. Juliá performed on the evenings when the play was presented in Spanish at the Astor Place Playhouse. He played the role of

Astolfo, the king's nephew. Performing in *La Vida Es Sueño* was especially important because it enabled Juliá to get his Actors Equity card from the union of professional actors. The card identifies holders as professional actors and makes them eligible for many theater jobs that are open only to union members. During this time he also got an agent. He hired Jeff Hunter to represent him. Their relationship would continue throughout Juliá's career.

At first, Juliá swallowed his pride and accepted an allowance from his parents so that he could make ends meet. But after he received the role of Conrad Birdie in *Bye Bye Birdie* in 1965, he proudly told his parents that he would be able to support himself. Getting good roles, however, was not always a sure thing. There were times when he wished he had waited before declining his parents' financial help.[9] According to Orvil Miller, a friend who also appeared in *Bye Bye Birdie*, Juliá began the habit of buying and storing canned food during this time—a habit he would have for many years as insurance for the times when money and food were not so plentiful.[10]

Juliá also joined Phoebe Brand's Theatre in the Street. This mobile theater company performed in both English and Spanish throughout New York City. It performed mostly in poor neighborhoods, like Bedford-Stuyvesant and Spanish Harlem, trying to bring theater to people who might not ordinarily be able to attend. The truck in which the actors and crew traveled turned into a stage, complete with lights and scenic backdrops.

In 1966, Juliá earned the part of Macduff in a mobile Spanish-language production of *Macbeth*. Later that same year and into 1967, he appeared in *The Ox Cart*. This drama, written by René Marqués, was about the difficult adjustment that a Puerto Rican family goes through when they move to the United States. The plot was not too different from what Juliá himself was experiencing. Juliá's performance did not escape the notice of theater critics, one of whom praised the "sustained intensity" of his portrayal of the adopted son Luis.[11]

Another actress who played alongside Juliá in The Ox Cart, Miriam Colón Valle, was dismayed that the important play was not reaching many Latinos in New York. A native Puerto Rican, Colón began to raise funds and soon was able to establish the Puerto Rican Traveling Theatre (PRTT). From the very beginning, the PRTT had three main goals: to present bilingual plays and emphasize the dramatic literature of Latin America; to promote the work of United States-based Latino playwrights; and to bring the theater to people who could not ordinarily afford it. With some modest initial funds, Colón's mobile theater began to perform in parks, playgrounds, and on streets throughout New

York City. Colón continues as the touring company's president today.

For a while, Juliá acted with the PRTT. Although he loved street theater, it was not always easy performing in the local neighborhoods. One time, when he was acting in the Bedford-Stuyvesant section of Brooklyn, New York, Juliá was lying on the ground, as the character he was playing was required to faint. All of a sudden, a bottle crashed on the ground next to his head. He yelled to the crew: "Hurry up and turn off those lights!"[12] Another time, in sweltering heat, he was dressed in a fancy Renaissance suit, singing Italian love songs. Before he knew it, an egg splattered against his costume. Juliá continued to sing, ignoring the egg that was dripping down his side. Yet another time, pranksters threw mattresses from a roof.[13] Carla Pinza, a Puerto Rican actress who worked with Juliá in several street theater productions, remembers: "Raúl wasn't street-smart the way American-born Puerto Ricans often are. He was naive [innocent] and had that wonderful quality that people from the island bring with them."[14]

Even still, Juliá always maintained that street theater was what inspired him most and called it a "fantastic experience." He said, "I want to feel an audience, and I am stimulated by *any* response they give me. . . . That's what it's all about. That's why we're up there on that stage in the first place."[15] When asked

Miriam Colón Valle established the Puerto Rican Traveling Theatre, which brings theater to people who could not ordinarily afford it.

about his relationship with the audience, Juliá said he had a difficult time putting his feelings into words. He did know, though, that he loved the way his acting could make people laugh or cry, move them, or inspire them. He felt that he became part of each person in the audience.[16]

Despite the hardships of street theater, Juliá was sure that "if you can play in the street, you can play anywhere. It is such a pleasure to see the bright faces of the children, many of them seeing theater for the first time."[17] Pinza remembered, "The children loved him. They would follow him offstage when he made his exit and ask him about the play. Raúl would explain what was going on and tell them to go back and watch the play and pay attention to what was happening on stage."[18] "It was a wonderful experience," Juliá later recalled. "We were bringing theater to people that had never gone to the theater before."[19]

In 1967, Juliá was performing in a Puerto Rican poetry reading at the Delacorte Theater. One of the people in the audience was Joseph Papp, the powerful producer and director of the New York Shakespeare Festival (NYSF). The NYSF produces plays every summer and puts them on free to the public, in Central Park.

That evening at the Delacorte, Juliá recited a patriotic poem with great emotion. Juliá said, "I really got into it and the audience stood up at the end and started cheering."[20] When he reflected later on that fateful evening, Juliá modestly admitted, "I guess he [Papp] saw some talent."[21]

Soon thereafter, Papp cast Juliá as Demetrius in the violent Shakespearean play *Titus Andronicus*, despite the fact that the Latino Juliá did not have the traditional looks for the part. "For me it was great," Juliá enthusiastically said, "because [Papp] saw through prejudice and stereotypes. He saw me, the talent that I had, my ability, and gave me the opportunity to use and develop it."[22] In the role of Demetrius, Juliá played a murderer who himself is killed, baked into a pie, then served to his mother. Juliá's involvement in *Titus Andronicus* was the first experience of what would turn out to be a long history with the New York Shakespeare Festival.

After his role in *Titus Andronicus*, Juliá was once again out of work. As Juliá put it, he was "broke and starving to death."[23] The unemployed actor decided to call Joseph Papp. He remembered the telephone call: "I didn't know if Papp remembered me. I didn't know him that well. I paced up and down in my apartment for a long time, to gather up the strength to call Joe Papp himself. In those days, it was like calling the pope. I said, 'I don't care what I do, as long as it's in the theater.'"[24] Juliá told Papp that he did not care what job he was given—he could even be a janitor. Then, he dramatically joked that he was ready to kill

In 1966, Raúl Juliá (second from right) was cast in the New York Shakespeare Festival's production of *Macbeth*.

himself because he was desperate to work in the theater. Papp replied, "Okay, don't commit suicide, it'll make a mess. Call me in about ten minutes."[25]

When Juliá called back, the director asked him if he had ever been a house manager. A house manager ensures that everything runs smoothly during a production. Juliá responded, "No, but I will be the best house manager you ever had."[26] Juliá immediately became the house manager for Papp's production of

Hamlet that played at the NYSF's downtown home, the Public Theater.

As the house manager for the New York Shakespeare Festival, Juliá put in many long hours, taking care of all the details that would ensure a smooth performance. But he thoroughly enjoyed his work and was even able to get some small parts in the productions. Said the actor, "To me, if nothing else had ever happened to me in my life, I would have been very happy working for the New York Shakespeare Festival. I practically lived there."[27]

Juliá always called Papp his mentor and credited Papp for giving him "the opportunity to play all those great roles."[28] Juliá explained: "Most producers and casting people don't see actors the way Joe Papp sees actors. He sees through them. There are a lot of people that see me just as a Hispanic. If it was up to those people, I would be playing Hispanics for the rest of my life."[29]

As the founder and director of the New York Shakespeare Festival, Joseph Papp was an influential figure in the New York theater scene. But many people felt that Papp thought of himself as overly important. Juliá disagreed, responding by saying, "Not so, not true. Joe knew what he was doing. Whether he got good reviews or bad reviews, the whole thing for him was that it was all—every bit of it, the sweet and the sour— a learning experience. I owe him so much, so much."[30]

Joseph Papp served as director of the New York Shakespeare Festival. He became a friend of Juliá's, and supported the talented actor's career.

During this time, Juliá married his fiancée, Magda Vasallo. When he left Puerto Rico in 1964, he was engaged to her, his childhood sweetheart, who was also his cousin. In Latin America, as in many parts of the world, it is not unusual for cousins to wed. They married in 1965 and stayed together during some of Juliá's most difficult times as an actor. But the union was not to last. The marriage ended in divorce in 1969.

Juliá then turned all his attention to developing his acting skills and to establishing his presence on Broadway.

CHAPTER FOUR

AN ACTOR'S LIFE

 When Raúl Juliá was once asked what his secret was for acting, he admitted he did not always know. "Sometimes it's an instinct," he said. "Sometimes it's an intellectual idea, and you have to be willing to make a fool of yourself." If asked to do something difficult, he would say, "I'll do it, and find out later if I [can] do it."[1] He found that thinking "Oh, piece of cake" was not nearly as exciting as "Ooh, wow, would I dare?"[2] "The more you're willing to make a fool of yourself," he declared, "the more space you open for brilliant things to happen."[3] It was precisely this

willingness and courage to try that led Juliá to play many different roles.

Juliá's Broadway debut came in September 1968, when he was selected to play Chan, a servant to a wealthy family in *The Cuban Thing*. To land the part of Chan, however, Juliá had to audition four times. Finally, having grown impatient with the play's producers, he burst out: "You know damned well that I'm the only one right for this role. Now make up your minds!"[4] Juliá eventually got the part, but the play unfortunately closed after only one performance. Juliá's talent was noticed by producers and directors, however, and he was called to play other roles.

The following year, 1969, Juliá was cast in the play *Indians*. This tragedy, written by Arthur Kopit, played at the Arena Stage in Washington, D.C. It tells about the devastation of American Indian people and their culture at the hands of Europeans. In this play, Juliá had an opportunity to demonstrate his versatile acting skills by playing three different parts: a Mexican Indian, a German actor, and a Russian grand duke. His talent was noted in many reviews by theater critics. The play was so costly to produce, however, that it closed after a few months.

In 1970, Juliá received the role of Paco Montoya in *The Castro Complex*. Even though the play received unfavorable reviews from critics, many felt that Juliá's performance provided "most of what small enjoyment" was to be found in the play.[5] In her review of the comedy, Marilyn Stasio remarked on Juliá's "strong presence" and "attractive stage personality." She closed her review by saying that Juliá "has a future— in better plays."[6]

Although he was fiercely proud of his heritage, Juliá was not content to merely play Latino characters. He declared, "I didn't come here to be Mr. Puerto Rican. I'm an actor. I'm not some stereotype."[7] Juliá was told that he would have an easier time if he changed his Spanish name to something more mainstream. He refused.[8]

During this time Juliá met a beautiful, dark-haired actress while rehearsing for an off-Broadway show. Her name was Merel Poloway and they soon entered a long-term, committed relationship. Juliá said of his beloved, "Merel and I are together. We *love* together."[9]

As Raúl Juliá's popularity increased on Broadway, Hollywood directors were taking note of the Puerto Rican actor. He appeared on the television soap opera *Love of Life* as well as the children's show *Sesame Street*. As people across the nation discovered the handsome young actor, they organized a fan club. Juliá even received several marriage proposals by mail from his most ardent fans.

Juliá did not particularly enjoy his time acting in the soap opera. In *Love of Life*, he played a Cuban immigrant escaping the dictatorship of Fidel Castro. He

Broadway is the theatrical district of New York City. Raúl Juliá made his debut on Broadway in 1968.

recalled with distaste how he had to repeat the same line over and over again: "'I love you and I want to tell your father.' It was terrible but I got so many letters. One was from a teenage girl who had been watching the thing for 12 years. Imagine, 12 years! Yuuck! It was the very pit of my life."[10] Juliá was glad when his character returned to Miami and he left the show.

During the 1971–72 season of *Sesame Street*, Juliá was part of the regular cast and played Rafael the Fixit Man. He also received small parts in three films: *The Organization, Been Down So Long It Looks Like Up to Me*, and *The Panic in Needle Park*. Although they were modest parts, they gave Juliá the experience of acting in films. But after so many months in front of a movie camera, Juliá was eager for a live audience once again.[11]

The opportunity came while Juliá was appearing on *Sesame Street*. This was when Joe Papp asked Juliá to appear in the role of Proteus in *Two Gentlemen of Verona*, for which he would receive his first Tony Award nomination. By 1972, Juliá had appeared on stage, in films, and on television.

Audiences, critics, producers, and directors were all taking note of the gifted actor. After only eight years of being in the United States, it could be said that Raúl Juliá was on a definite path to stardom.

A RISING STAR

Raúl Juliá was a natural on the stage and screen. Theater and movie critics often praised his talent. One writer said, "Onstage, his style is charged. He's got a sonorous [vibrant] voice and the kind of physical presence you can't learn." A film producer agreed: "He's got incredible dash and flair and sex appeal."[1] Many people commented on the electricity that Juliá seemed to radiate. One newspaper reporter wrote, "Raúl Juliá gives off energy the way some people perspire, and just as involuntarily."[2]

When Juliá appeared in *King Lear* in 1973, his portrayal of the scheming Edmund was called "deliciously conniving."[3] That same year he was also cast in the major role of Orlando in *As You Like It*, another Shakespearean play. In all, Juliá would act in over a dozen Shakespearean productions. Juliá said of the playwright: "I revere Shakespeare. I love the rhythm, the music, the poetry. I make it my own . . . become a poet . . . and I just see Shakespeare smiling at me."[4]

In 1974, Juliá received his second Tony Award nomination for his role in *Where's Charley?* In this musical comedy, Juliá played the title role of Charley Wykeham, an English college student who impersonates his aunt. Although he did not win the Tony that year, Juliá would have plenty of opportunities in the coming years to try again.

During this time, Juliá became involved with a self-help movement called est. Est was founded in California in 1971 by Werner Erhard. Est means "it is" in Latin and also stands for Erhard Seminars Training, named after its creator. It is usually written in lowercase letters to emphasize its modesty and simplicity.

The training seminars were conducted in large urban cities and would accommodate large numbers of people at a time. By 1991, more than seven hundred thousand people had participated in Erhard's seminars, paying $250 to $625 each. Its popularity was due, in part, to the many celebrities that had taken the training: Valerie Harper, Diana Ross, Cher, Yoko Ono, Cloris Leachman, Ted Danson, and Roy Scheider, among others. The late singer/songwriter John Denver even dedicated an album, *Back Home Again*, to est and wrote a song, "Looking for Space," as a tribute to the training. Denver believed in est so strongly that he claimed he wanted to give up singing to work for the organization.[5]

From the beginning, a lot of mystery surrounded the movement. One major question asked was what it was supposed to be. The est leaders alleged that it was a training that was philosophical in nature. Some critics called it brainwashing, although most agreed that that would be too strong a claim. Others declared that it was a religion. Most felt that it was a type of psychotherapy designed to help people gain more control over their own lives. Estians claimed that the training would enable people to derive more satisfaction from life. Graduates reported greater success, health, and happiness.

Part of the mystery resulted from the fact that trainees were requested not to reveal to nongraduates the contents of the est training. Of the little information that did leak out, it was disclosed that the sessions were highly structured. People were told when they could talk, drink, eat, and go to the bathroom. The intensive training would take place over two consecutive weekends, for fifteen to eighteen hours each day. Some feel

Juliá brought incredible energy and passion to each role that
he played.

that these strict rules made the training that much more effective.

Another source of controversy was the founder's background. Werner Erhard had held a number of different jobs—in an employment agency, in a meatpacking plant, as a sales manager in the automobile business, and as an office manager for an encyclopedia company. However, he soon developed a reputation for being honest, hardworking, and very effective at personnel training.

In any event, Juliá attended the est seminars and credited them with a renewed sense of purpose and energy. He and Poloway experienced the self-fulfillment philosophy for the first time in 1974 after a friend told them about it. They each became passionate supporters of the program. In turn, Erhard attended a performance of *The Threepenny Opera* in which Juliá was starring. Soon, Juliá, Poloway, and Erhard became friends. They even traveled together on a spiritual journey to India.

On several occasions, Juliá credited his theatrical success to est, saying that it had "been an important contributor."[6] In several theater programs, Juliá chose to mention est rather than his acting credits. In the playbill for *The Threepenny Opera*, Juliá included the following saying from est:

> Man keeps looking for
> a truth that fits his reality.

Given our reality,

the truth doesn't fit.

If you experience it,

it's the truth.

The same thing believed

is a lie.

In life,

understanding is the booby

prize.[7]

To one reporter, Juliá explained, "All I can say is that it [the est experience] was fantastic. Est taught me I have everything inside me."[8]

In *The Threepenny Opera*, Juliá played the role of the sinister Macheath, sometimes also called Mack the Knife. Assuming a flawless British accent, Juliá had to project charm and evil at the same time. He played the starring part so well that when British theatergoers met him backstage, they were astonished to hear Juliá's natural Latin accent when he spoke.[9]

Juliá's portrayal of Macheath was so accomplished that at least one critic called him "the casting coup of the season." Another said, "He's got to be considered one of the half-dozen best classical actors in the country." Yet another likened him to a bomb that never explodes.[10] The comparison pleased Juliá: "I really liked that comment about the bomb ready to explode at any moment. What I'm trying to do is to *keep* a high level of tension in my performance, to keep up a sense of tense, neurotic discomfort. It's easy for an actor to explode. What's hard is to keep from exploding."[11]

For his excellent acting in *The Threepenny Opera*, Juliá received his third nomination for the Tony Award but unfortunately did not win.

In 1976, Juliá and Merel Poloway were married by the Indian Swami Baba Muktananda at a spiritual retreat in the Catskill Mountains. Even though neither of the two were Muktananda's disciples, Juliá and Poloway respected the guru, who had been introduced to them by Erhard. Years earlier, Juliá's mentor Joe Papp had been blessed by Muktananda with a peacock feather. Juliá called the wedding "beautiful" and was especially pleased that their friends and families were able to attend: "Our parents were there, our families, everybody sitting on the floor throwing rose petals at us."

The year 1977 proved to be an important one in Juliá's life. In that year the actor learned about The Hunger Project, which was created by Werner Erhard, the founder of est. Erhard claimed that the terrible poverty and starvation he saw while on the trip he made to India with Juliá was the motivation to establish The Hunger Project.[12] The project announced that its goal was the elimination of world hunger and starvation by the year 2000. It was based on the belief that humans produce enough food to feed everyone in

J uliá was dedicated to working for The Hunger Project from its creation in 1977 until his untimely death. He is pictured speaking at the Hunger Project's worldwide teleconference in 1987.

the world but that politics and distribution problems prevent that undertaking. Juliá said,

> I was involved from the beginning. It came out of the realization that for the first time in the history of this planet, we had the means to end hunger, and all that was needed was to make it a priority.[13] When I found out in 1977 that we have the technology to end hunger on the planet, I had to get involved.[14]

The project earned almost instant popularity. Within two months of the project's founding, thirty-six thousand people had attended Erhard's presentations on world hunger.[15] Juliá was so committed to the project that in 1982 he called it "the most important thing for me at this moment"[16] and insisted that statements on behalf of the project be inserted into the stage programs for the shows in which he was performing.

In 1978, Juliá was selected to play the title role in *Dracula* when the lead actor who had been playing the vampire left the show. Juliá accepted the part and received much acclaim from theater audiences. During this time, he also began rehearsing for his role as Petruchio in *The Taming of the Shrew*, which would play on Broadway. Because *Dracula* was playing at the John F. Kennedy Center in Washington, D.C., Juliá had to commute to New York several times a week to practice with his costar, Meryl Streep.

At first, his meetings with Streep did not go well. Streep recalled how frightened she was of him: "Everything about him was so big—his eyes, his gestures, his smile—and he was so loud, and I was terrified of him."[17] Caught up in the moment of an intense scene during a rehearsal, Streep attacked Juliá with her fingernails. He fought back by stabbing her arm with a pencil point. When she tried to remove the point and was not able to, Juliá said: "Aha! Now you'll never get rid of me!" As their friendship developed, the actress was glad she had a permanent reminder of Juliá.[18]

When Joe Papp saw Juliá in the finished production of *The Taming of the Shrew*, he compared the actor with the great, magnetic stage actors of the past. Said the Broadway director:

> When I saw him in that performance, I thought he began to show himself as one of the major actors in this country. The stance, the whole bearing and the kind of easiness, the kind of life that he has inside of him which is quite extraordinary. . . . I saw this happening over the past few years, but I'd never seen it so completely realized as when I saw him out there.[19]

From there, Juliá accepted a role in a movie being shot in Italy. When he received the script for the Broadway show *Nine*, he was in Rome filming the movie *Tempest*. Because Italian director Federico Fellini's film *8 1/2* was the inspiration for the play *Nine*, Juliá used the opportunity to study Italian culture while he was in Rome to prepare for his role. During his several-month stay in Italy, he also arranged to have dinner with Fellini so that he could better understand the role.

Nine turned out to be both personally and commercially rewarding for Juliá. It was a lavishly choreographed production that was physically tiring for Juliá, whose lead role kept him onstage for most of the play. He received his fourth Tony Award

Juliá poses against a stage poster for the Broadway play *Nine*,
for which he received his fourth Tony Award nomination.

nomination for his performance. Although he never actually won a Tony Award, he was content with just getting nominated and recognized for his work. "There's something beyond winning or losing," he said, "which is just celebrating."[20]

While *Nine* received a total of twelve Tony Award nominations, many critics considered Juliá "indispensable" and commented that "few performers can carry that kind of weight."[21] When it was reported that he was being paid $15,000 a week plus 1.5 percent of the profits, Juliá was deeply embarrassed. He asked, "Who wants the world to know how much money you make?"[22]

One of the reasons why Juliá was able to command such a high salary was because of his growing popularity with moviegoers. The 1980s were already proving to be a great decade for the Puerto Rican actor in both theater and motion pictures.

CHAPTER SIX

HOLLYWOOD!

One characteristic that made Raúl Juliá such a special talent is that there was no such thing as a typical Raúl Juliá role. One writer marveled that Juliá was one of a "rare breed of working actors who can move effortlessly and without vanity from one project to the next, stage to screen, leading roles to character parts."[1] Joe Papp once said of his protégé: "He was always outrageous in his acting choices. He's larger than life all the time when he's on the stage. He doesn't mind falling flat on his face doing something dangerous."[2] His movie career was turning out to be as diverse as the one he was cultivating on Broadway.

In 1982, Juliá appeared in a modern film version of Shakespeare's *The Tempest*. Juliá played the part of Caliban, a bawdy and funny goatherd on a Greek island. The movie centers on an accomplished New York architect who is disgusted with his boring life. He escapes by going to a Greek island and trying to live an existence that is far removed from modern life. Most critics liked the adaptation, citing Juliá's amusing portrayal as "side-splitting."[3] Reviewer Robert C. Trussell wrote that Julia's acting is "a show-stealing performance that dominates the film."[4]

The following year, Juliá and his wife, Merel, experienced an exciting event: the birth of their first son, Raúl Sigmund. They were overjoyed, and Juliá was glad he had waited to have children until his career was established and stable.[5]

Perhaps the most important film for Juliá was *Kiss of the Spider Woman* (1985). It was significant for several reasons. The movie was based on a novel written by the Argentine author Manuel Puig. In the movie, Juliá plays the political prisoner Valentín, who shares a jail cell with a flamboyant gay man named Molina, played by William Hurt. Valentín has been imprisoned because of his communist beliefs and is tortured because he refuses to betray his comrades. To pass the time, Molina tells fanciful stories about the fantastic Spider Woman. As time passes, the seemingly dissimilar prisoners become friends and end up making huge sacrifices for each other.

Juliá, Hurt, the director, and the screenwriter were all so impressed with the project that they agreed to postpone their pay just to get the movie made. Juliá felt that it was one of the best scripts he had ever read, saying, "It is so rare, either as an actor or as a film-maker, to come across a project of such depth and such humanity. So we took a chance."[6] They all agreed that if, by chance, the movie turned out to be a hit, they would collect their salaries plus a percentage of the profits.

To study for his part as the Marxist revolutionary, Juliá met with rebels in South America. He asked them about their beliefs and their lives. He also met ex-prisoners who had been, like Valentín, tortured. Explained Juliá: "I wanted to be a person who is willing to go through pain and torture for what he believes."[7] At first, he had wanted to play Molina, saying that he thought the role was "more meaty." Soon, however, he reported, "I'm very happy with Valentín. As it turned out, after the research that I did and working on the part, I just love the part."[8] One critic felt that in *Kiss of the Spider Woman*, Juliá did "his best movie work ever."[9]

To sharpen their acting, Juliá and Hurt switched their roles one day on the set. This is a rehearsal technique that actors often use. On the day of the role reversal, the film crew stopped working to watch, they were so captivated by the performance.

Kiss of the Spider Woman was unusual in that the actors were allowed one full month to rehearse. Most movie actors do not have such a luxury. Juliá recalled that there was no pressure on the production: "We went down there and we had as much time as we liked. We rehearsed for four weeks! We worked it and worked it until we were satisfied."[10]

Juliá was also pleased that the film was shot in sequence. Usually, scenes in movies are filmed out of order for a variety of reasons. Juliá liked that he grew as his role developed and that he did not have to shoot the end first. "It's much harder that way [to shoot out of sequence] because you have to imagine it. You have to work on a scene as if [earlier events] had happened. When you shoot it chronologically, it really did happen already."[11]

In order to look more the part, Juliá lost thirty pounds. He said, "I learned from my research that there are no fat revolutionaries."[12] He joked that the hardest part "was watching everybody eat this delicious Brazilian food. I never saw so many great snacks and meal breaks."[13] Working on the film was very intense, since the crew worked together six days a week, twelve hours a day, for four months. By the time the filming was wrapped up, Juliá said, "I felt like I was getting out of prison myself."[14]

When it was released, critics praised the film lavishly. Even more surprising was that it became a huge hit commercially. When it opened in New York, the ticket lines wrapped around the block for over a month. Said a pleased Juliá,

> I knew it was a good film, a very special film, but I didn't expect this kind of intense response. I thought it would be a more specialized audience—you know, art-film people—but I am very pleasantly surprised that more people are getting it. I think there is a hunger for this kind of artistic experience, to be moved in a profound way, a human way.[15]

One newspaper reporter wrote, "The lesson about generosity and goodness touched audiences around the world."[16]

Although most critics highly praised Juliá's acting, Hurt received the bulk of the accolades. Hurt won the best actor award at the Cannes Film Festival, which is held every spring in France. When Hurt later won the Academy Award for Best Actor, Spain's "Pantalla Dorada" (Golden Screen) objected, saying that Hurt had played his part of a South American gay man weakly, without so much as even a trace of a Hispanic accent. They felt that Juliá's acting was superior and the awarding unfair. Juliá did, however, receive a Golden Globe nomination, and the National Board of Review awarded their best actor prize to both Juliá and

Hurt. To Hurt's credit, when he accepted the Oscar for Best Actor at the Academy Awards, he accepted the award in both his and Juliá's names.

Even though the commercial success was nice, Juliá always felt that it was not as important as the artistic challenge and importance of a project. Joe Papp said of his student, "Raúl has never pursued commercial alternatives in an aggressive way. He loves the theater, and that part has always mattered more to him than the pay. I used to have to kick him out to go make money, so that he could live comfortably."[17]

Immediately after wrapping up *Kiss of the Spider Woman*, Juliá played detective David Suárez opposite Susan Sarandon in *Compromising Positions*. This movie was very different from the film he had just completed. *Compromising Positions* was a romantic mystery-comedy in which a housewife (Sarandon) investigates the murder of a local dentist with the help of a handsome detective (Juliá). It offered Juliá a mental and physical break from the difficulties of *Kiss of the Spider Woman*.

In 1986, Juliá played opposite Jane Fonda in the thriller *The Morning After*. Although he had already been in twelve films up to this point, audiences really started to take notice of the actor. He played the role of Fonda's ex-husband and Beverly Hills hairdresser, Joaquín "Jacky" Manero. To prepare for his part, Juliá spent time in beauty salons, took lessons, and even worked at the Vidal Sassoon hair salon in Los Angeles. Juliá joked, "I learned how to set hair and cut hair . . . if I'm ever out of a job, I can do it."[18] Even though his character did not occupy a lot of screen time, Juliá's portrayal left "a firm impression in the audience's mind of his character's determination to make something of himself in a prejudicial society."[19]

Also in 1986, Juliá costarred in the first full-length movie made in Puerto Rico. It was a Spanish-language film called *La Gran Fiesta (The Big Party)*. The film's producers billed it as Puerto Rico's entry into world cinema. The movie is about a colorful ball with a subplot of businessmen and government officials trying to influence politics. Juliá makes a grand, but brief, appearance as an eccentric poet. Most critics hailed the film, citing the excellent performances and quality of the camera work and production.

In 1987, Juliá traveled to Mexico to film *The Penitent*. In a movie about religious fanaticism, Juliá plays a hardworking peasant who is selected to represent Christ in an annual ritual. Every year someone is chosen to be tied to a cross in a simulation of Christ's death. Usually, the chosen one dies the way that Christ did. The movie was not very popular with theater audiences, but Juliá was very proud of the film, and considered its quality to be on the same level as *Kiss of the Spider Woman*.[20]

Juliá's family was a great joy in his life. He cherished time spent with his wife, Merel, and sons Benjamin Rafael (left) and Raúl Sigmund (right).

Whenever possible, Juliá was eager to work with Latino filmmakers. He said of the Latino community, "We have numbers on our side. Already we are an economic power, and a growing one. Someday, everyone will realize it."[21] The actor Ricardo Montalban agreed, saying: "At first, for a long time, screen Hispanics were bandits or lovers. Then we were ignored. Today we are underrepresented, and often misrepresented, but due to our increasing numbers, we are ignored less and less."[22]

That same year, 1987, Juliá's second son, Benjamin Rafael, was born. Juliá now had two sons, and the boys quickly became the center of his attention. His friend Lilian Hurst said that he always showed his kids' photos with great pride to anyone who would look. Hurst says, "His great love was his children. Raúl sometimes felt bad that he was away from his children when he was on tour or shooting a film. He wanted to take his kids with him but was also conscious that he did not want to disrupt their lives and childhoods."[23] Another of Juliá's friends, the actor Edward James Olmos, agreed that "Raúl's family filled his heart."[24]

Juliá was very active between 1987 and 1989. When *Variety* published its list of the busiest Hollywood actors, Juliá's name was at the top. For the first time, Juliá started to receive starring roles, rather than merely supporting ones.

Nonetheless, not all his acting parts were well-received. Most critics felt that Julia's talent was wasted in *Moon Over Parador* (1988), when he played a corrupt South American police chief, Roberto Strausmann, who was of German descent. For the part, Juliá had to bleach his naturally dark hair to make it blond. Although the cast was made up of talented veterans such as Juliá, Richard Dreyfuss, and Sonia Braga, and was directed by Paul Mazursky, the movie failed to please audiences and most film critics.

In 1989 Julia starred in *Romero*, a film about Archbishop Oscar Arnulfo Romero who was assassinated in 1980 while delivering mass in a church in El Salvador. Romero was a target because he was so outspoken about human rights violations in the region. His assassins were never brought to justice. Juliá accepted the role precisely because of its political content, wishing to draw attention to problems in Central America. The actor acknowledged that the role itself is the most important thing to consider when choosing which film to do. He felt that some roles, like that of Romero, "have to be done."[25]

Juliá was widely acclaimed for his sensitive portrayal of the archbishop. It was obvious that the film transformed him; he said that it had been a "profound" experience.[26] To prepare for the part, Juliá read Romero's autobiography and his personal diary, listened to some of his sermons that were on audiotape, and watched some videotapes of the archbishop saying mass. Juliá took his role seriously, saying, "I had a responsibility to do justice to this man, this hero, this giant, this saint."[27]

Because El Salvador was engaged in a bloody civil war that took the lives of seventy-five thousand people, it was too dangerous to film *Romero* on location. The movie was instead shot in Mexico. When the movie was released, the Salvadoran government prohibited its showing in El Salvador. Still, many videos were secretly circulated, and El Salvadorans watched the movie clandestinely in private homes.

Romero was also important to Juliá for a more personal reason. As an adult, Juliá had drifted from his boyhood religion of Catholicism. In studying for his part and in acting the role of Archbishop Romero, Juliá rejoined his faith. The actor admitted that making the film became an experience for him of personal conversion. Juliá confessed that before filming *Romero*, he had had mostly negative feelings about the Catholic Church and had felt that it did not contribute positively to people's lives. But while he was filming in Mexico, he said that he saw for the first time how the church worked with the poor and how it "did make a difference." These experiences caused Juliá to reevaluate his own relationship with God. He later wrote of his experience in *Sojourners*, a religious magazine.[28]

In 1989, Raúl Juliá starred in the movie *Romero*, about a priest who was assassinated in El Salvador. Portraying the martyred priest was a deeply moving experience for Juliá.

The movie's producer, Ellwood "Bud" Kieser, was also a Paulist priest. The Paulist order of the Catholic Church is dedicated to tending to those outside the church. The film has the distinction of being the first commercial film financed, in part, by the Catholic Church. During the course of the film shoot, Kieser held four masses. At night, after putting in a full day on the set, Juliá and Kieser would spend hours in deep, spiritual discussions. After the experience, Juliá returned to his childhood faith and attended Catholic mass regularly.

In 1990, Juliá played the Argentine-Jewish lawyer Alejandro "Sandy" Stern in *Presumed Innocent*. The movie is a murder mystery set mostly in the courtroom, where Juliá's character expertly defends his client Rusty Sabich, played by Harrison Ford. As with all the other roles he had accepted, Juliá spent quite a bit of time studying his character's background, beliefs, and values. To prepare for the part, he spent days with a criminal attorney and sat in on cases in court to become more familiar with the court system, court-room manners, and how lawyers act and talk. He saw many parallels between theater and law: "Lawyers are frustrated actors. As a matter of fact, a lawyer I spoke to said the performance is more important than any-thing else."[29]

The long hours of study paid off for the actor. Most critics found that the defense attorney in *Presumed Innocent*, who managed to rise above the corrupt legal system, was played particularly well by Juliá. One reviewer said, "Juliá plays him with a pleasing suave [gracious] dignity."[30] Another critic wrote that Juliá gave the screen performance of his career and got "closer to the manner of a big-time lawyer than any other actor I can recall."[31]

In 1991 Juliá received the news that his longtime mentor, Joseph Papp, had died at the age of seventy from cancer. Many movie and theater stars, including Meryl Streep, Al Pacino, Robert De Niro, and Juliá attended Papp's large funeral in New York. Juliá mourned the loss of his friend, saying, "I miss him, man, I miss him. [I] think about him a lot. I talked to him just before he passed away."[32]

Papp was instrumental in casting Juliá in a variety of roles, not just those that were Latino. Juliá felt a need to always work against being typecast. Although it still happens today, Latino movie stars of earlier decades had an even more difficult time. Fernando Lamas, who died in 1982 in his mid-sixties, once said, "I have been very lucky. I always knew I had little talent. But I came along early enough so my type ["Latin lover"] was still in vogue, and from my type, I made a career."[33] Juliá refused to play a formulaic "type." He declared, "I'd rather not work than be typecast and do the same things over and over."[34] "I like variety," he explained. "I don't like to play the same type of role over and over again. The more different the better."[35]

Unfortunately, Juliá always had to fight against being seen only in ethnic terms. He complained, "It is a barrier, a hindrance. Hispanics are as varied as North Americans."[36] Juliá was once being considered for a movie that he felt had one of the best movie scripts he had ever read. Although he did a great audition, the director (whose name Juliá refused to disclose) eventually gave the part to a more traditional-looking "white" actor.

Juliá felt that Hollywood was filled with filmmakers who did not want to cast a Latino actor in a non-Latino role. He praised Joe Papp for "taking chances, going beyond normal, beyond safe" and lamented that he had not "met a Joe Papp in film yet. I don't know if there is one."[37]

Unfortunately, many directors took one look at Juliá and thought that he was only capable of playing ethnic characters. He was also frustrated that film executives predictably funded movie projects that were not always high quality. Juliá felt that the entertainment industry often treated audiences as if they were stupid and unable to understand films that represented the depth of human emotions. It was this very depth and variety of human experience that Juliá felt people craved.

Juliá's goal was always to be a multifaceted classical actor, to be able to play many different types of parts. When he played an Italian car-racing champion, in *Gumball Rally*, he said: "That's what I love. . . . It's great, all those changes—from an Italian lover to Macheath to *Where's Charley?* Incredible!"[38] When asked to take on a difficult role, his response was to plunge in. "That's what I like about this business," he said. "I can go from one world to another. That's what makes it interesting."[39]

Of all the films Juliá was in, he may be best known for his portrayal of Gomez Addams in *The Addams Family* (1991). In this film, based on Charles Addams's gruesome but lovable cartoons, Gomez is the patriarch of a humorously morbid family. Juliá was drawn to the part because he felt "Gomez is like a kid in a candy store. Everything is wonderful. Even his depressions are wonderful."[40] "Besides," explained the actor, "it's a relief to play [a character like] Gomez. As rewarding as dramas are, the comedies need to be a part of the mix. I'm so serious in so many of my films . . . it's fun to romp in the fields once in a while."[41] Barry Sonnenfeld, the movie's director, said: "Raúl was born to play Gomez. He loves his wife, he loves his children, he loves life. He loves acting."[42]

Scott Rudin, the producer of the film, first cast Anjelica Huston for the part of Gomez Addams's wife, Morticia. When he turned his concern to casting the male lead, he said, "Once you had Anjelica, once you have a racehorse like her, you have to have someone opposite her who's got equal power. You've got to have the Raúl Juliás of the world, and suddenly you've got a style piece."[43] Huston agreed to play Morticia while she was having breakfast with Sonnenfeld and Rudin. Suspiciously, she asked, "Who are you thinking of for Gomez?" When they replied, "Raúl Juliá," she enthusiastically cried, "Perfect!"[44]

Many special effects were used to create the $30 million movie. Several scenes were added during the filming, others were omitted, and some were not even created until the movie was almost finished. It took 106 days to shoot and many months to edit.

In the television series, Thing, the disembodied hand, was never out of the box it lived in. But in the movie, Thing was played by the real right hand of magician Christopher Hart. Hart would make his hand jump, scurry, and run. Hart's body was erased through trick photography. For a few scenes, Thing is played by a plastic hand. In one scene, Gomez uses Thing for a golf tee. "Raúl swung and broke the fingers off the first hand we built," explained the film's special effects designer. "I don't think Chris [Hart] would have enjoyed that much."[45]

The movie proved to be a hit with audiences, especially with younger viewers. A sequel was made in 1993, *Addams Family Values*, that some people found funnier than the original. The plotline of the sequel involved the birth of another baby for Morticia and Gomez. Moviegoers roared with laughter as the Addamses tried to find a competent nanny for their baby, who had a premature mustache.

In 1992, Juliá was cast as Don Quixote in Cervantes' *Man of La Mancha* on Broadway. Juliá was especially pleased because the part had originally been played by José Ferrer, one of Juliá's childhood idols.

The musical first opened on Broadway in 1965 and is the ninth longest running musical in American theater. Placing his hand on his heart, Juliá proclaimed: "Cervantes is Spain's Shakespeare."[46] Juliá identified with Don Quixote, a dreamer who envisioned himself performing heroic deeds. Juliá said: "We all have Don Quixote inside of us. We are all dreamers. We would all like to see a better world. We all would like to make a difference."[47]

Man of La Mancha proved to be a challenge for Juliá. The show's schedule required him to perform eight times a week. Although he sang well, he had not been trained as a singer. Consequently, he had not learned how to protect his vocal chords. He soon took the advice of a musical conductor and a friend and started wearing warm scarves, warming up his voice before the show, and gargling with vinegar and honey.

Sometimes critics ridiculed Juliá's Shakespearean performances, saying that he was "too ethnic." With his dark Latino looks and his rich voice, which always retained the accent of his native Spanish, some critics felt he was improperly cast to play classically English Shakespearean roles. When mixed reviews were printed, Juliá would feel hurt and upset. He admitted, "Sometimes, without wanting to, I would find myself with the temptation to do what the reviewer said, just because of the power of the printed page."[48] So Juliá's solution was simple: he stopped reading the reviews.

Even though his agent tried to persuade him to speak more like English actors, Juliá refused, pointing out, "Shakespeare is more universal than people try to make him."[49] When the part required it, Juliá was able to slip into whatever accent was necessary. In Harold Pinter's play *Betrayal* (1980), Juliá played an Englishman with the appropriate upperclass English accent, after spending several weeks in London and hiring a coach. One theater critic noted that Juliá was a "marvel of professional finesse."[50] Still, another proclaimed that Juliá had been "ethnically miscast."[51] Soon, however, his superior acting skills forced critics to "rethink the possibilities for classic acting."[52]

In 1994, Juliá played the role of Chico Mendes in the HBO movie *The Burning Season*. The movie tells the story of Mendes, a Brazilian laborer who went on to organize people in an effort to stop the destruction of the Amazon. Mendes was eventually murdered on his doorstep in 1988 at the age of forty-four. Although the assassins were caught and sentenced to nineteen years in prison, they escaped after serving only three years and have never been found.

Juliá learned about Mendes by reading interviews and studying film documentaries of the Xapuri Rubber Tappers' Union, which Mendes had founded. The Xapuri were the indigenous people who lived and worked in the forest. Juliá was very impressed with Mendes's courage. "That's what makes a hero," the actor said; "someone who actually makes a difference."[53] Juliá said of Mendes: "He was just a regular guy, full of life and its enjoyment. The film shows how a human being under the right circumstances has a choice, to make a difference beyond himself or to retreat."[54] Critics widely praised Juliá's performance, calling it "riveting," "searing," and "perhaps his best performance ever."[55]

Although the story takes place in the Amazon, *The Burning Season* was actually filmed in a privately owned jungle in Mexico. The chosen site was easier to film in than the Amazon, but the temperature still reached as high as 107 degrees. During one scene that took place in the headquarters of the workers' union, fifty to sixty people were crowded in the enclosed room. No fans or air-conditioning could be run because of the noise that they would produce. It was all the cast could do to finish the scene. Every time the director yelled "Cut!" everyone would rush outside to get a breath of fresh air. Juliá admitted that at times it was difficult to keep up his energy, "but in a way, the heat was in keeping with the film."[56] Movie director John Frankenheimer got the film shot in six weeks, a very short amount of time by movie industry standards.

Kamala López-Dawson, the actress who played the part of Mendes's wife, Ilzamar, says that working with Juliá was a wonderful experience. She remembers that

Actress, screenwriter, and film producer Kamala López-Dawson was Juliá's co-star in *The Burning Season*.

Juliá was extremely generous with compliments, something that is not always typical of movie stars:

> I once had a suggestion during the shooting of the film, but I was uncomfortable telling it to the director. So I told it to Raúl. Raúl thought it was a good idea and later relayed it to John [the director]. John decided to do it, saying that it was brilliant. Raúl agreed that it *was* brilliant, but quickly and publicly pointed out that it was my idea.[57]

López-Dawson also remembers Juliá's lavish praise during one scene where several of the movie's characters, including her, are sitting around a table. For the scene, a close-up had to be taken of each actor. After the close-up of López-Dawson was taken, Juliá complimented her on being such a "wonderful actress" and found her portrayal "extremely moving." The praise meant a lot to López-Dawson, since it was coming from such an accomplished actor. She was also pleased that at a surprise birthday party that was thrown for her during the shooting, Juliá sang. It is a special memory for her.

One day toward the end of the filming, someone from the crew proposed a trip to a local hotel and seafood restaurant on the coast that he had heard about. Juliá, who loved sushi (a raw seafood dish), and a few of the crew and cast took off for a seafood dinner. By the time they returned to camp, they were all sick. Although everyone else got better, Juliá

Juliá, a naturally exuberant person, is pictured at Kamala López-Dawson's birthday party.

worsened. Some feel that his condition was aggravated by an earlier stomach operation he had had in January. He had to be airlifted to Mexico City to receive medical treatment.

When he returned, he was thinner and frail-looking. One of his costars, the Brazilian actress Sonia Braga, remembers that despite his weakened condition, Juliá never complained. She remembers, "We'd be sitting on the beach and he'd be talking to everybody, telling jokes and singing songs."[58] Some feel that he should have taken a longer time to recuperate. Between the stomach surgery and the food poisoning, Juliá had lost forty-five pounds. But he was anxious to get to his next project, a film based on the video game *Street Fighter*.

Kamala López-Dawson remembers that he was looking forward to doing *Street Fighter* because it would provide the opportunity to spend time with his sons, who could provide him with their perspectives on the game. Even though the film was a very strenuous project for Juliá, López-Dawson felt that he accepted the role for his kids, whom he loved very much and who often served as an inspiration to him.

Little did they all know that this would be the last major film Juliá would work on.

THE FLICKERING
STAR

Life seemed good to Raúl Juliá in 1994. At the age of fifty-four, he was an established Broadway actor. He had several film credits that had earned him popularity in the United States and abroad. He had continued to live in Manhattan, close to the theater life he loved. He and his wife, Merel Poloway, lived in a comfortable New York apartment with their two sons, Raúl Sigmund and Benjamin Rafael. On the weekends, they would all travel to the Catskill Mountains to their country home. A few times a year, Juliá and his family would visit relatives in Puerto Rico.

Juliá was a Catholic; Merel, a Jew. They made sure that their two sons received instruction in both religions. The important decision about which faith to follow was left up to the boys when they got older. Juliá, who had strayed from Catholicism as an adult, had returned to his boyhood faith during the filming of *Romero*.

After shooting *The Burning Season* in the summer of 1994, Juliá traveled to Australia and Thailand to film *Street Fighter*. The action hero of the movie, Colonel Guile, was played by Jean-Claude Van Damme. Juliá's sons, Raúl and Benjamin, who loved the video game, were excited that their father was going to play the villain. They even helped him prepare for his part.

To play the role of the evil General M. Bison, Juliá drew upon his Shakespearean training. General Bison is determined to conquer the world, and Juliá felt that the role was in the classic villain tradition of Richard III.[1] To make him look even more evil, the lighting was cast from below to accentuate his cheekbones and huge eyes. Most critics felt that although the movie itself was not very good, Juliá's performance was excellent. One reviewer wrote, "The actor gives it his all, widening his eyes into an electric glare of cartoonish ferocity, swishing his cape and cackling fiendishly."[2]

Juliá (right) is pictured relaxing on a boat with his co-stars, Edward James Olmos and Sonia Braga, from *The Burning Season*. After shooting on that movie wrapped up in 1994, Juliá traveled to Australia and Thailand to film *Street Fighter*.

In his military costume, Juliá looked particularly thin. His family explained that he had undergone surgery on his intestines earlier in the year that had resulted in a great loss of weight.[3] For the most part, his family kept his medical condition private. But some friends felt that Juliá "knew he did not have much time left."[4]

On the evening of October 16, 1994, Juliá and his wife attended a performance at the Metropolitan Opera House in New York City. Poloway later commented on the happiness that the two felt in sharing the evening together.[5] Of her husband, Poloway once said, "I like everything about Raúl, good and bad. I like his vitality, his openness, his warmth."[6] After the performance, the two made their way home, as Juliá had an interview scheduled with Marcos Zuriñaga, the Puerto Rican film director responsible for *Tango Bar*.

But despite the appearance of good health, Juliá began to feel ill. He began to experience a strong pain in his stomach and called an ambulance. The actor was seemingly not too worried about his condition because he was seen reading over the script for his next movie, *Mariachi*. To show his positive spirits, he even sported one of his many police hats that he collected when he was admitted to the hospital. When Zuriñaga arrived at Juliá's home, he learned that the actor had been taken to North Shore University Hospital in Manhasset, Long Island. The film director arrived at the hospital and was told that Juliá was going to be kept for observation.

At 4:00 A.M., Juliá suffered a stroke. During a stroke, a blood vessel in the brain bursts, causing a hemorrhage in the brain. The condition is severe, oftentimes resulting in death. His agent, Jeff Hunter, said that the stroke "was totally unexpected."[7] His wife, Merel, and his personal assistant, Susan Wright, stayed close by, watching anxiously.

At first, there was guarded optimism about Juliá's condition. His doctors said that there was a very good chance the actor would recover. Soon, however, it was clear that the actor's state was deteriorating. He fell into a coma on Thursday, October 20, 1994, and did not regain consciousness. With his family watching helplessly by his bedside, Juliá was placed on life support. The actor died at 11:48 in the morning the following Monday, October 24, 1994, at the age of fifty-four, from complications resulting from the stroke he had suffered.

There had been rumors that Juliá had had brain cancer and that the tumor was what caused the stroke.[8] Several writers reported that he had been battling cancer for months. These reports were never confirmed. The actor's cousin, Carlos Juliá, emphatically denied the rumors, explaining that brain hemorrhages were fairly common in the family. Both Juliá's father and grandfather had died of the same cause. Zuriñaga reported that Juliá's doctors believed the strong stomach pains indicated that intestinal bleeding had occurred, which, in turn, sparked the brain hemorrhage.[9]

In accordance with his wishes, Juliá's body was taken to Puerto Rico. Very quickly a state funeral was arranged for October 27 in San Juan. When the American Airlines flight that carried Juliá's bodily remains landed at Luis Muñoz Marín Airport, it was met by sixteen motorcycle escorts. As the motorcade

Family was always an important part of Juliá's life. He is pictured here with his sister María Eugenia (left), mother Olga (center), and sister Olga María (right).

made its way through the streets, hundreds stood by, watching the somber parade. The governor of Puerto Rico, Pedro Rosselló, proclaimed three days of mourning, during which the flags of the United States and Puerto Rico would be flown at half-mast.

As in many Latin countries, a wake was held in Juliá's honor. It was held at the Instituto de Cultura Puertorriqueña (Institute of Puerto Rican Culture) in Old San Juan. A wake is a time for the friends and family of a deceased person to grieve and pay their respects before the burial. Thousands waited patiently to walk by the actor, who was lying in state and whose coffin was covered with red roses and the flag of Puerto Rico. During the four hours that the institute was open to the public, Puerto Rican *plenas* (folkloric music) played in the background. One of Juliá's cousins played the guitar, while old friends from the University of Puerto Rico sang in homage. Merel, accompanied by her two sons, Raúl, age eleven, and Benjamin, age seven, expressed how grateful they were at the display of love: "He [Raúl Juliá] felt that in a certain way, the whole island was his family. Wherever he went he sang songs of Puerto Rico. Thank you very much for the love you have for him."[10]

The morning of the funeral was a rainy one. Thousands attended the event and lined the streets of San Juan, shielding themselves from the rain with umbrellas, newspapers, and even pieces of carpet. As the coffin was being loaded into the hearse, singer Lucesita Benítez sang the Puerto Rican hymn "La Borinqueña." As the song ended, a woman shouted "Bravo! Bravo, Raúl! Bravo!" The crowd erupted into applause.

The funeral procession then went on to Juliá's boyhood school, Colegio San Ignacio de Loyola. As the procession made its way through the streets, workers came out of their offices, flags on their buildings at half-mast, to wave good-bye. Children threw flowers. Many held signs that read "We love you."

More than fifteen hundred people went to the service held in the San Ignacio de Loyola Church, which is located next to the school. The headmaster of the school, Reverend Juan Santiago, asked the crowd to say good-bye to Juliá in a manner consistent with his theatrical background: "Let us say farewell to Raulito with applause, the way we would in a theater."[11] The crowd got to their feet and applauded for more than two minutes.

Under a torrential downpour, the group made its way to Buxeda Cemetery in Río Piedras, where Juliá would be buried. The Puerto Rican senator for the Independence Party, Rubén Berríos Martínez, who had been a school friend of Juliá's, offered the final words. "Raúl came to this world to make us more happy. He never had enemies, he was a true star, in the sense of the light that radiated from him and his work. That is why today Puerto Rico is darker."[12] Berríos likened Juliá to a "luminous [glowing] mirror in which Puerto Ricans see the best of themselves."[13] Juliá's widow, overcome with grief, alternately looked at Berríos Martínez and at the coffin, scarcely understanding what was being said.[14] Also in solemn attendance were Juliá's mother, Olga Arcelay, and his two sisters, María Eugenia and Olga María, who had flown in from

Mexico City and Valencia, Spain, respectively. As the coffin was lowered, shouts from the crowd could be heard: *"Viva Puerto Rico Libre!"* ("Long live a free Puerto Rico!") and *"Viva Raúl Juliá"* ("Long live Raúl Juliá!") as white carnations were dropped from a helicopter overhead. Juliá was buried alongside his father, Raúl, and brother, Rafael. Family members asked that instead of sending flowers, contributions could be made to The Hunger Project or the New York Shakespeare Festival as Juliá would have wished.

Memorial services were also held in New York City on November 6 at the Joseph Papp Public Theater. In addition to the hundreds of fans that attended, many movie stars paid their respects and sang Juliá's praises. In attendance were Meryl Streep, Susan Sarandon, Bud Kieser, and Juliá's old acting coach Wynn Handman. As the theater began to fill with people, television monitors were set up in other rooms to accommodate the growing crowd. Latecomers listened to the proceedings on loudspeakers outside or in the lobby.

Streep recounted the story of how she had scratched Juliá when they had acted together in *The Taming of the Shrew* sixteen years earlier, and how she was glad that he had left a permanent mark on her arm. She said that he "emanated exuberant joy" on which she and others had come to depend "like heat in winter."[15] Arthur Kopit, who wrote the play *Indians* in which Juliá performed, remembered the actor as "the greatest appreciator of anything. He would cry out ardently, 'What a sky!' or even 'What cornflakes!'"[16] William Hurt, who was not able to attend in person, nonetheless, delivered a speech by video. He remembered his time with Juliá as "full of feeling and joy, pondering, dancing and singing." He also said that he played many games of chess with his friend, which Juliá "always generously won."[17]

Services were also held in Los Angeles on November 9. Fellow actors Rubén Blades, Edward James Olmos, Laura Dern, and others spoke of Juliá's warmth, talent, and legacy in making the world a better place. Several film clips highlighting the actor's career were also shown. It was announced that *Street Fighter*, Juliá's final screen performance, would be dedicated to him.

In Miami, a church service was held at the Corpus Christi Church in a neighborhood where many Puerto Ricans live. Victor Ramas, a Puerto Rican activist, said, "He deserves this. We want people to know that we love him, that he is an idol, and that he is a positive image for us. This [his death] is something hard to accept. It makes me proud to see how far he had gotten."[18]

In addition to formal memorial services, many friends of the late actor organized smaller, more intimate observances. Actress Carla Pinza, Juliá's lifelong friend, organized a vigil. With candles in hand, a procession walked from Saint Agnes Boys High School in Manhattan to Juliá's home between 86th and 87th streets. With a shaky voice, Pinza recited a poem by Luis Llorens Torres that was one of Juliá's favorites.

One month after Juliá's death, the actor was honored at a Puerto Rican festival held in Bayfront Park in Miami. Salsa bands from Puerto Rico, New York, and South Florida played from 1:00 to 9:00 P.M. Just as the sun began to set, a moment of silence was observed in Juliá's memory, and the song *"En Mi Viejo San Juan"* ("In My Old San Juan," one of Juliá's favorites) was sung.

After Juliá died, his friends at the New York Shakespeare Festival placed a memorial in the trade paper *Variety*. The simple remembrance in the lower right-hand corner of the page listed his birth and death years and quoted a Shakespearean passage:

> His life was gentle, and the elements
> so mix'd in him that nature might stand up
> and say to all the world, "This was a man!"[19]

The verse was a fitting tribute to a modest, elegant man driven by humanitarian ideals. Not just the theatrical world, but all humanity suffered a great loss the day Raúl Juliá died.

ACTIVIST AND
ROLE MODEL

Raúl Juliá was considered to be a man of strong humanistic beliefs. He was involved in various political and social causes to better the condition of people all over the world. He asserted, "If you think something is wrong, do something to change it."[1] Scott Rudin, the producer of *The Addams Family*, appreciated Juliá's ability to have both a social conscience and, at the same time, a "sense of fun."[2] Joe Papp always admired that in addition to being a fine actor, Juliá was consistently "a very fine, gentle, feeling person."[3]

Juliá maintained his sense of personal responsibility throughout his life. Unlike most celebrities, he refused the sheltered, protected life that many movie stars lead. He once said,

> People tend to become elusive, you know; people tend to hide in their caves when they become stars. They create for themselves these very wonderful, comfortable caves with a few of their tribe around, and they stop participating in life and with people. I don't intend to do that—I like to participate and I don't want to lose that.[4]

Despite his stardom, Juliá did not surround himself with bodyguards, and he good-naturedly signed autographs for people he met on the street. He was a favorite for interviewers, who described him as "passionately low-key," "all energy and no edge," and "surprisingly egoless" for an actor.[5] Juliá's longtime friend, Lilian Hurst, feels that one of his most attractive traits was that "his fame never went to his head."[6] Another of his friends, Rubén Berríos Martínez, insists that Juliá is the only person he ever met who did not have any enemies. Despite Juliá's stardom, Berríos Martínez says, "he stayed the same, in his generosity, in his simplicity, in his total absence of pretense."[7]

Along with Merel and their two sons, Juliá was very active in The Hunger Project. He believed that Americans thought hunger was only a problem in developing countries. "We seem to find the poverty in other countries, but we don't see the poverty that's around the corner here. There are people going hungry in the cities in this country—elderly people, young people that are going hungry by the thousands every day."[8] To demonstrate his dedication, Juliá fasted one day a month and donated those meals to a food bank. He made appearances on radio and television on behalf of The Hunger Project and narrated video programs in both English and Spanish for the organization. Even with an exhausting stage and screen schedule, Juliá raised funds by speaking at many benefits around the country. In 1992 he received the first Global Citizen Award from The Hunger Project.

Shortly before his death, Juliá had taken out several full-page ads in *The New York Times* and *The New York Daily News* conveying the message that all people needed to unite to win the war against hunger. In the acknowledgments of *Ending Hunger: An Idea Whose Time Has Come*, Juliá and his family were recognized for their contributions to The Hunger Project. After his death, the organization set up The Raúl Juliá Ending Hunger Fund and promised to "use these funds with the kind of creativity, boldness, and effectiveness that Raúl would have wanted."[9]

Juliá's dedication to human rights and social causes prompted him to become involved in a number of activities and organizations. In 1994, he participated as an observer in the Salvadoran elections to ensure that they were conducted in a fair and democratic manner. He was part of the official delegation sent by Freedom House, a human rights organization based in New York, to supervise the elections. This trip was especially important to Juliá because, although he had played Salvadoran Archbishop Romero in 1989's *Romero*, this was the first time he had set foot in El Salvador. He was deeply moved by his visit to the chapel where Romero was assassinated, to his grave, and to the place where he was born. He was heartened that a semblance of peace had finally been restored to the country.[10] Upon his return to the United States, Juliá wrote an article for *Freedom Review* describing his experience and expressing hope for future peace in El Salvador.

In addition to having filmed *Romero*, one of Juliá's last acting projects was the cable movie *Down Came a Blackbird*. It was shown for the first time on the cable channel Showtime after Juliá's death. The film is about the horrors of political torture and the deep wounds that it leaves on its victims. In it, Juliá plays a doctor named Tomás Ramírez who, as he helps torture victims, reveals his own dark secret. Working on the film further emphasized to Juliá the importance of making people aware of political and human rights violations throughout the world. The film was finished just six days after Juliá died.

R aúl Juliá (far right) was an observer at the 1994 elections in
El Salvador to help ensure that they were conducted fairly
and democratically.

Another social issue that was of significance to the actor were the problems that confronted young people. Juliá was involved in a number of youth-oriented programs. Concerned with the rising frequency of violence among teens, Juliá cosponsored a script-writing competition among high school students. He urged teens to communicate their feelings through art rather than through violence. He told them, "If you want to express your anger, write it down. If you want to murder your father or throw your mother out the window, write it down—because then it becomes art instead of tragedy."[11] As a tribute to his efforts on behalf of young people, a new elementary school in the Bronx was dedicated as the Raúl Juliá MicroSociety Dual Language School in June 1996.

After his death, the Puerto Rican Family Institute, an agency that provides social and mental health programs in the United States and Puerto Rico, sponsored a black-tie dinner in honor of the actor. In attendance were Rosie Pérez, a Puerto Rican actress, and Joseph Unanue, the president of Goya Foods, a company that makes Hispanic foods. Held at the Plaza Hotel in New York City, tickets cost $350 per person and proceeds were used to fund programs for Puerto Rican families that Juliá would have supported.

Juliá has served as a role model for countless actors, who saw his performances in over thirty plays and films. Helen Hunt, the actress best known for the

TV series *Mad About You* and the movie *Twister*, remembers seeing Juliá and Meryl Streep in *The Taming of the Shrew* in Central Park when she was thirteen. Thereafter, she became obsessed with Shakespeare.[12]

Juliá advised hopeful young actors to persist in their dream. Focused work, determination, and risk taking, Juliá recommended, are the secrets of success. "Sometimes it is a temptation to blame luck for your failure," warned Juliá. "But you create your own situations. You get results by your own efforts. Not necessarily hard, driving, exclusive effort, but continued effort, relaxed concentration, gearing everything you do to your goal. Persistence pays off."[13]

For Latino actors, Juliá was especially inspirational because of the wide range of roles that he played throughout his thirty-year professional acting career. As Nancy Rosado Camacho put it, "He opened doors so that others could step through."[14] Lilian Hurst considers Juliá a role model. She even displays a photo of him in her home, which she considers "indispensable." Hurst also remembers how Juliá always tried to help others in the profession. When the Puerto Rican actress auditioned for a part in *The Cuban Thing*, Juliá was instrumental in helping her get the part. He was already cast and was watching Hurst's audition. Suddenly, the play's producer asked Hurst, "Do you have an agent?" Newly arrived, Hurst did not have an agent and did not know how to respond. Out of the corner of her eye, she saw Juliá nodding to her. She responded to the producers' question by saying yes. "OK, then," said the producers, "who is it?" Hurst gulped, not knowing what to say. Juliá quickly scribbled the name and telephone number of his own agent, Jeff Hunter, on a piece of paper and handed it to her. Because of Juliá's quick thinking, Hurst got the part.[15]

In a tribute to Juliá after his death, author Laurie Winer wrote: "It's safe to say that Raúl Juliá made a difference to any young Latino actor dreaming of the stage, because his dignified presence effectively banished any lingering 'Bab-a-loo!' stereotyping."[16] Juliá once asserted:

> I'm willing to play any role, including a Latin role, if it's well written. I will not play a Latin stereotype. And most of the roles that are written about Latins in this country are stereotypes, roles that have no profundity [depth], or no knowledge or no humanity. They're just very general people. They don't have any challenge for me.[17]

To help other Latino actors, he was active in the Hispanic Organization of Latin Actors (HOLA). HOLA promotes Latino talent in the American theater and develops theater in Spanish. Juliá was also a cofounder, with Carla Pinza, of *Visiones Luminosas* (Shining Visions), an organization established to promote Latino screenwriters. Latino directors recall how

Juliá's widow, Merel, and sons accepted the 1995 Hispanic Heritage Award in the late actor's honor. Presenting the award was Juliá's friend Edward James Olmos.

many times Juliá charged very little for his work, or not at all. The actress Elia Enid Cadilla cannot recall one time when Juliá rejected a project that had to do with Puerto Rico or Puerto Ricans.[18] During Puerto Rico Discovery Week in New York City, Mayor Rudolph Giuliani presented a special proclamation to Juliá's family, naming November 21, 1994, Raúl Juliá Day.

Alberto Minero, once the director of the Americas Society Theater, remembers how quickly Juliá responded to his request to be involved in a Latino talent show. Juliá was finishing a project in Canada and was on his way to Brazil to film *Kiss of the Spider Woman*. Juliá, nonetheless, made time to appear in the program, informing Minero that he would be interpreting two poems by Federico García Lorca. Minero later recalled how Juliá's presence and passion gave the poems an emotion that Minero had never witnessed before.[19]

As a tribute to Juliá and to his commitment to young Latino actors, the Puerto Rican Traveling Theatre set up two tuition-free educational programs. The Raúl Juliá Training Unit offers aspiring young actors the opportunity to perfect their talent. The Playwrighting Unit helps develop new Latino playwrights and writers. More than five thousand students have gone through the programs, and many have gone on to achieve national recognition.

Juliá made no effort to disguise the fact that the theater was his first love. "For me," he said, "Hollywood was, like, doing something else in between doing theater."[20] He compared the theater to standing on a mountaintop and shouting your confession; whereas a film allowed a more secret, whispered disclosure. He especially enjoyed the closeness that develops between an actor and the audience during a performance. He once said, "That feeling is unique, of sharing the experience and getting the reaction, or not getting the reaction. It's incredible. It's there, it's happening right there. And it's gone forever after it's gone."[21] Juliá saw theater acting as a bigger risk and challenge than acting in movies. He acknowledged, however, that experiences in the theater contributed to success in motion pictures, and vice versa. "My ideal," he said once, "is to come and go between the theater and film."[22] In January 1996 Juliá was inducted into the Theatre Hall of Fame at the Uris Theatre on Broadway.

In his effort to bring theater to people who might not ordinarily have the opportunity to attend it, Juliá never lost his interest in mobile theaters. He also accepted roles in New York Shakespeare Festival productions in Central Park without getting paid. "Acting is about giving," he once said in an interview. "The greater the acting, the greater the giving."[23] His commitment also led him to serve on the board of directors of the New York Shakespeare Festival, the advisory board of the National Theater of the Deaf, and the New York Council for the Humanities.

Throughout his life, Juliá was intensely proud of his Puerto Rican heritage. He once pointed out, "When the Pilgrims arrived at Plymouth, our capital was one hundred years old. We already had a culture."[24] His wife, Merel, confirmed that he "cherished his Hispanic roots."[25] Although he had many Puerto Rican friends who were from New York, he pointed out, "I didn't grow up in El Barrio. I am from the island."[26] In fact, one close friend teased that Juliá wore the map of Puerto Rico on his forehead: "He wanted everyone to know he was Puerto Rican."[27]

The political status of Puerto Rico has always been a source of controversy. Some people feel that it should continue to be a colony of the United States. Others believe that becoming the fifty-first state of the United States would be best for the island. But Juliá, like many others, felt that it should become a free and independent republic. The actor voiced this opinion on many different occasions.

Whenever he had the opportunity, Juliá traveled to his homeland. He was a spokesman for the Puerto Rican Tourism Company, beckoning travelers to come and experience the beauty and warmth of his homeland. He also helped independent Puerto Rican filmmakers by appearing in their films for free or for a modest fee. A project that Juliá was working on when he died had the working title "Puerto Rico in Hollywood." On the island, a twelve-hundred acre rain forest has been named for the beloved actor.

One year after his death, Julia's widow and sons accepted a Hispanic Heritage Award in his honor. This is one of the most prestigious awards in the Latino community. The awards were established to recognize creative and dedicated Latinos in the areas of education, literature, leadership, and the arts.

The black-tie gala event was held at the National Building Museum in Washington, D.C. There were one thousand guests in attendance. Juliá's friend and fellow actor Edward James Olmos presented the organization's first posthumous award. Said Olmos, himself a 1992 award recipient: "Raúl was one of the most extraordinary artists of our time, and I'm honored to be asked to be here. His passing has left us longing too soon. We've lost a giant and a genius. Imagine, here was a man who could do Shakespeare in two languages!"[28] Olmos told an interviewer that a long time would pass before another actor would rise to an international level the way Juliá did.

That same year, 1995, Merel accepted a posthumous Emmy Award, Cable Ace Award, and Golden Globe Award in her husband's name for his portrayal of Chico Mendes in *The Burning Season*. Juliá also received the Best Actor award from the Screen Actors

Guild. After receiving one of these awards, his widow said: "These events make you feel great. That mitigates [softens] the sense of loss. He would've been so honored if he were here. It's weird to go around the country and pick up awards for him, but I try to bring him around with me inside, into the present."[29] When Olmos received his 1995 Golden Globe Award for best supporting actor, the audience grew somber when he dedicated it to the memory of Juliá.

In Miami, the Puerto Rican Chamber of Commerce, in conjunction with other organizations, has established the Raúl Juliá Scholarship Fund. The organizers hope to collect $100,000 within the first five years to distribute to twenty low-income families with teenagers who want to pursue a college education. Alberto Ibargüen, the master of ceremonies for the 1997 opening event, said, "The lesson that Raúl Juliá taught us is the lesson of community. He was a Puerto Rican actor that never lost sight of where he came from. He was a human being that concerned himself with those who were less fortunate than he. He was an actor and a teacher."[30]

Juliá prided himself on being an ambassador of ethnic harmony. "In a way, I'm like an instrument to dissipate prejudice. I love to meet prejudiced people. I can clear up their prejudices, just by talking to them, showing them what a Puerto Rican is really like."[31] His desire to stamp out prejudice, in part, led him to become involved in Racial Harmony, an organization dedicated to promoting interethnic understanding. He soon became the chairman of the Joseph Papp Celebrity Coalition for Racial Harmony.

Even though Juliá was very proud of his Latino identity, most of his friends and admirers feel that his appeal was more universal. Said his childhood friend Rubén Berríos Martínez: "His roots were in Puerto Rico, but the tree was very big."[32]

Edward James Olmos said:

> For me, Raúl Juliá is the greatest actor of the century. He was Puerto Rican in origin, but universal in his work. In terms of artistic versatility, he was greater than Olivier, Hoffman, Pacino, Nicholson, and De Niro. Each of these actors has, without a doubt, great moments in their respective film careers. But, I ask: Could any of them dance and sing with the passion and precision with which Raúl did on stage?[33]

To chronicle his achievements, an independent film company is working on developing a documentary on his life titled *Raúl Juliá: Esta Es Su Vida (Raúl Juliá: This Is His Life)*. The film will be released in both English and Spanish versions.

Juliá once said: "I'll do anything as long as it's something I can get value out of. It doesn't have to be a heavy, soul-searching thing as long as it is something that has some beauty, some quality. I think everything I've done has had that."[34] One of Juliá's friends insists that the actor "came to this earth so that human beings, particularly Puerto Ricans, would be happier."[35] Through his theatrical work, Juliá brought laughter and emotion to many people. Through his humanitarian efforts, he brought comfort. The world is a better place because Raúl Juliá was once in it.

Selected Theater and Film Credits

THEATER PLAYS

Life Is a Dream (La Vida Es Sueño) (1964)

Bye Bye Birdie (1965)

Macbeth (1966)

Titus Andronicus (1966 and 1967)

The Ox Cart (1967)

No Exit (1967)

The Memorandum (1968)

The Cuban Thing (1968)

Illya Darling (1968)

Your Own Thing (1968)

The Hide and Seek Odyssey of Madeleine Gimple (1968)

Indians (1969)

City Scene (1969)

The Persians (1969)

The Castro Complex (1970)

Two Gentlemen of Verona (1971)

Hamlet (1972)

King Lear (1973)

As You Like It (1973)

Where's Charley? (1974)

The Emperor of Late Night Radio (1974)

The Robber Bridegroom (1974)

The Threepenny Opera (1976)

The Cherry Orchard (1977)

The Taming of the Shrew (1978)

Dracula (1978)

Othello (1979)

Betrayal (1980)

Nine (1982)

Design for Living (1984)

Arms and the Man (1985)

Man of La Mancha (1992)

FILMS

Stiletto (1969)

The Organization (1971)

Been Down So Long It Looks Like Up to Me (1971)

The Panic in Needle Park (1971)

The Gumball Rally (1976)

The Eyes of Laura Mars (1978)

The Escape Artist (1982)

The Tempest (1982)

One From the Heart (1982)

Overdrawn at the Memory Bank (1984)

Kiss of the Spider Woman (1985)

Compromising Positions (1985)

Mussolini: The Untold Story (1985)

The Morning After (1986)

Florida Straits (1986)

La Gran Fiesta (1986)

Trading Hearts (1987)

Tango Bar (1987)

The Alamo: 13 Days to Glory (1987)

Moon Over Parador (1988)

Tequila Sunrise (1988)

Onassis: The Richest Man in the World (1988)

The Penitent (1988)

Romero (1989)

Mack the Knife (1989)

Havana (1990)

Presumed Innocent (1990)

The Rookie (1990)

Frankenstein Unbound (1990)

A Life of Sin (1990)

The Addams Family (1991)

The Plague (1992)

Americas (narrator) (1992)

The Monkey People (narrator) (1992)

Addams Family Values (1993)

The Burning Season (1994)

Down Came a Blackbird (1994)

Street Fighter (1994)

CHRONOLOGY

1940—Born on March 9 as Raúl Rafael Carlos Juliá y Arcelay in San Juan, Puerto Rico.

1964—Moves to New York City to pursue his career as an actor; debuts in the Off-Broadway production of *La Vida Es Sueño.*

1965—Appears in *Bye Bye Birdie*; marries Magda Vasallo.

1966—Meets Joseph Papp and begins a long association with the New York Shakespeare Festival; is cast in NYSF's production of *Macbeth* and *Titus Andronicus*; is cast as Luis in *The Ox Cart* alongside Miriam Colón Valle who gets the idea to establish the Puerto Rican Traveling Theatre.

1967—Plays Demetrius in *Titus Andronicus*; is cast as Cradeau in *No Exit.*

1968—Juliá travels with the road company production of *Illya Darling*; makes his Broadway debut in *The Cuban Thing*; appears in the satire *The Memorandum.*

1969—Appears in *Paradise Gardens East* and *Conerico Was Here to Stay*; appears in *Indians* at the Arena Stage in Washington, D.C.; divorces Magda Vasallo.

1970—Plays a revolutionary fugitive in *The Castro Complex*; appears in *Sesame Street* as Rafael the Fixit Man.

1971—Wins fame in *Two Gentlemen of Verona* on Broadway, for which he receives Tony Award nomination; appears in *The Organization, Been Down So Long It Looks Like Up to Me*, and *The Panic in Needle Park*.

1972—Plays Osric in *Hamlet* while simultaneously appearing in *Two Gentlemen of Verona*.

1973—Plays a conniving Edmund in *King Lear* and as Orlando in *As You Like It*; appears in NYSF's *King Lear*.

1974—Earns his second Tony Award nomination for *Where's Charley?*; appears in the plays *The Emperor of Late Night Radio* and *The Robber Bridegroom*.

1976—Plays Mack the Knife in Broadway's *The Threepenny Opera*, for which he receives his third Tony Award nomination; plays an Italian racing car driver in the movie *The Gumball Rally*; marries dancer-actress Merel Poloway.

1977—Plays a Russian peasant in *The Cherry Orchard*; gets involved with The Hunger Project.

1978—Has the lead role in a road company production of Dracula; stars opposite Meryl Streep in *The Taming of the Shrew*; plays a villain in the film *The Eyes of Laura Mars*.

1979—Plays leading role in NYSF's production of *Othello*.

1980—Plays an Englishman in *Betrayal*.

1982—Plays a film director in *Nine*, for which he receives his fourth Tony nomination; appears in the movies *The Escape Artist, One From the Heart*, and a modern version of *The Tempest*.

1983—Son Raúl Sigmund is born.

1984—Plays a playwright in *Design for Living*.

1985—Plays the political prisoner Valentín in *Kiss of the Spider Woman*; plays Sergius in *Arms and the Man* on Broadway; appears in *Compromising Positions* as a police detective.

1986—Appears in *The Morning After* and *Florida Straits*; makes a cameo appearance as an eccentric poet in *La Gran Fiesta*.

1987—Appears in *Trading Hearts* and *The Alamo: 13 Days to Glory*; stars in *The Penitent*; second son Benjamin Rafael is born.

1988—Has supporting roles in *Moon Over Parador* and *Tequila Sunrise*; films the television miniseries *Onassis: The Richest Man in the World*.

1989—Plays Salvadoran Archbishop Romero in *Romero*.

1990—Stars in *Havana*; *The Rookie* (with Sonia Braga); *Frankenstein Unbound*; plays lawyer Sandy Stern in *Presumed Innocent*.

1991—Juliá's longtime friend and mentor, Joseph Papp, dies; plays the macabre Gomez Addams in *The Addams Family*.

1992—Stars in Broadway's *Man of La Mancha*.

1993—Plays Gomez Addams in the sequel *Addams Family Values.*

1994—Stars in HBO's *The Burning Season*; participates as an observer in the Salvadoran elections; completes filming of the movie *Street Fighter*; plays in *Down Came a Blackbird*; dies on October 24 in Manhasset, New York.

1995—Receives posthumous Hispanic Heritage Award, Emmy Award, Cable Ace Award, and Golden Globe Award.

CHAPTER NOTES

CHAPTER 1

1. Guy Flatley, "Raul Julia—The Man You Love to Hiss," *The New York Times*, December 26, 1971, p. 5D.

2. Frank Pérez and Ann Weil, *Raul Julia* (Austin, Texas: Raintree Steck-Vaughn, 1996), p. 25.

3. William A. Raidy, "'Now' Generation Matinee Idol," *Philadelphia Inquirer*, April 9, 1972, p. 2D.

4. Flatley, p. 5D.

5. Rebecca Stefoff, *Raul Julia* (New York: Chelsea House Publishers, 1994), p. 43.

6. Pérez and Weil, p. 27.

7. Phoebe Hoban, "Meeting Raul," *New York*, November 25, 1991, p. 52.

8. Clive Barnes, "Keach and 'Hamlet' Light Up the Park," *The New York Times*, June 30, 1972, p. 22L.

9. Ibid.

CHAPTER 2

1. Lois Athey, *Latin America* (New York: Globe Book Company, Inc.), 1987, p. 147.

2. Phoebe Hoban, "Meeting Raul," *New York*, November 25, 1991, p. 55.

3. Kevin Kelly, "The New Man of La Mancha," *Boston Globe*, March 8, 1992, p. 38B.

4. Ibid.

5. Jerry Parker, "Raul Julia: An Actor Who Does It All," *Philadelphia Inquirer*, September 8, 1982, p. 5C.

6. Allan Wallach, "The Evolution," *Newsday*, October 29, 1978, p. 4.

7. Guy Flatley, "Raul Julia—The Man You Love to Hiss," *The New York Times*, December 26, 1971, p. 5D.

8. Wallach, p. 4.

9. Hoban, p. 55.

10. Carolyn Beach, "Stardom Beckons Raúl Juliá," *Nuestro*, December 1985, p. 12.

11. Parker, p. 5C.

12. Ross Westzsteon, "Raul Julia Is a Sexual Time Bomb," *The Village Voice*, June 14, 1976, p. 141.

13. "The Unofficial Raul Julia Page" (on the Internet at http://www.pratique.fr/~docbrown/).

14. Frank Pérez and Ann Weil, *Raul Julia* (Austin, Texas: Raintree Steck-Vaughn, 1996), p. 12.

15. Burt A. Folkart, "Raul Julia: Actor Portrayed a Wide Array of Characters on Stage, Screen," *Los Angeles Times*, October 25, 1994, p. 20A.

16. Flatley, p. 5D.

17. Stephen Hunter, "Raul Julia: Despite Hit, He Faces Actor's Unsure Future," *Baltimore Sun*, September 8, 1985, p. 1G.

18. Parker, p. 5C.

19. Flatley, p. 5D.

20. Personal interview with Lilian Hurst, October 29, 1996.

21. Pérez and Weil, p. 15.

22. Susan King, "'Spider Woman' Part Gives the Kiss of Success to Raul Julia," *Los Angeles Herald Examiner*, August 27, 1985, p. 6C.

23. Kelly, p. 38B.

24. Hoban, p. 55.

CHAPTER 3

1. Guy Flatley, "Raul Julia—The Man You Love to Hiss," *The New York Times*, December 26, 1971, p. 5D.

2. Anna Quindlan, "Raul Julia—Out of the Ethnic Trap," *The New York Times*, July 10, 1977, p. 5D.

3. Rebecca Stefoff, *Raul Julia* (New York: Chelsea House Publishers, 1994), p. 28.

4. Flatley, p. 5D.

5. Ibid.

6. Personal interview with Lilian Hurst, October 29, 1996.

7. Burt A. Folkart, "Raul Julia: Actor Portrayed a Wide Array of Characters on Stage, Screen," *Los Angeles Times*, October 25, 1994, p. 20A.

8. Eric Pace, "Raul Julia Is Remembered, With All His Panache," *The New York Times*, November 7, 1994, p. 12B.

9. Jerry Parker, "Raul Julia: An Actor Who Does It All," *Philadelphia Inquirer*, September 8, 1982, p. 5C.

10. Norman Nadel, *New York World Journal Tribune*, December 26, 1966, as quoted in *Current Biographies*, 1982, p. 188.

11. Flatley, p. 5D.

12. Allan Wallach, "The Evolution," *Newsday*, October 29, 1978, p. 4.

13. Frank Pérez and Ann Weil, *Raul Julia* (Austin, Texas: Raintree Steck-Vaughn, 1996), p. 18.

14. Flatley, p. 5D.

15. Polly Anderson, "Raúl Juliá . . . Se Va Para Siempre en el Esplendor de su Fama," *El Vocero*, October 25, 1994, p. 39.

16. Flatley, p. 5D.

17. Pérez and Weil, p. 19.

18. Ibid.

19. Phoebe Hoban, "Meeting Raul," *New York*, November 25, 1991, p. 55.

20. Susan King, "'Spider Woman' Part Gives the Kiss of Success to Raul Julia," *Los Angeles Herald Examiner*, August 27, 1985, p. 6C.

21. Parker, p. 5C.

22. Carolyn Beach, "Stardom Beckons: Raúl Juliá," *Nuestro*, December 1985, p. 12.

23. William A. Raidy, "'Now' Generation Matinee Idol," *Philadelphia Inquirer*, April 9, 1972, p. 2D.

24. Hoban, p. 55.

25. Wallach, p. 5.

26. Hoban, p. 55.

27. Stefoff, p. 36.

28. Mel Gussow, "Raúl Juliá, Broadway and Hollywood Actor, Is Dead at 54," *The New York Times*, October 25, 1994, p. B10.

29. King, p. 6C.

30. Kevin Kelly, "The New Man of La Mancha," *Boston Globe*, March 8, 1992, p. 38B.

CHAPTER 4

1. Mel Gussow, "Raúl Juliá, Broadway and Hollywood Actor, Is Dead at 54," *The New York Times*, October 25, 1994, p. 10B.

2. "The Eyes Had It," *People*, November 7, 1994, p. 127.

3. Allan Wallach, "The Evolution," *Newsday*, October 29, 1978, p. 4.

4. Rebecca Stefoff, *Raul Julia* (New York: Chelsea House Publishers, 1994), p. 37.

5. Gussow, p. 10B.

6. Marilyn Stasio, *Cue*, November 28, 1970, as quoted in *Current Biographies*, 1982.

7. Scott Cain, "Raul Julia Makes Himself Known," *The Atlanta Journal*, January 9, 1986, p. 1P.

8. Phoebe Hoban, "Meeting Raul," *New York*, November 25, 1991, p. 54.

9. Guy Flatley, "Raul Julia—The Man You Love to Hiss," *The New York Times*, December 26, 1971, p. 5D.

10. William A. Raidy, "'Now' Generation Matinee Idol," *Philadelphia Inquirer*, April 9, 1972, p. 6D.

11. *Current Biographies*, 1982, p. 188.

CHAPTER 5

1. Phoebe Hoban, "Meeting Raul," *New York*, November 25, 1991, p. 54.

2. Anna Quindlan, "Raul Julia—Out of the Ethnic Trap," *The New York Times*, July 10, 1977, p. 5D.

3. Philip Elmer-DeWitt, et al., "Chronicles: Milestones," *Time*, November 7, 1994, p. 23.

4. Allan Wallach, "The Evolution," *Newsday,* October 29, 1978, p. 5.

5. Lisa Schwarzbaum, "Est! est! est!: How I Got It, How I've Kept It, and Why I Won't Go Back for More," *Mademoiselle*, October 1975, p. 174.

6. Jerry Parker, "Raul Julia: An Actor Who Does It All," *Philadelphia Inquirer*, September 8, 1982, p. 5C.

7. Ross Westzsteon, "Raul Julia Is a Sexual Time Bomb," *The Village Voice*, June 14, 1976, p. 140.

8. Ibid.

9. Rebecca Stefoff, *Raul Julia* (New York: Chelsea House Publishers, 1994), p. 50.

10. Westzsteon, p. 140.

11. Ibid.

12. Steven Pressman, *Outrageous Betrayal* (New York: St. Martin's Press), p. 164.

13. Hoban, p. 56.

14. Burt A. Folkart, "Raul Julia: Actor Portrayed a Wide Array of Characters on Stage, Screen," *Los Angeles Times*, October 25, 1994, p. 20A.

15. William Warren Bartley, *Werner Erhard: The Transformation of a Man: The Founding of est* (New York: Clarkson N. Potter Publishers, 1978), p. 255.

16. Parker, p. 5C.

17. Eric Pace, "Raul Julia Is Remembered, With All His Panache," *The New York Times*, November 7, 1994, p. 12B.

18. Ibid.

19. Wallach, p. 4.

20. Frank Pérez and Ann Weil, *Raul Julia* (Austin, Texas: Raintree Steck-Vaughn, 1996), p. 44.

21. Dick Lochte, "Nine," *Los Angeles Magazine*, April 1983, p. 58.

22. Parker, p. 5C.

CHAPTER 6

1. Frank Bruni, "Actor Tried, Mastered Many Roles," *Detroit Free Press*, October 25, 1994, p. 1A.

2. Burt A. Folkart, "Raul Julia: Actor Portrayed a Wide Array of Characters on Stage, Screen," *Los Angeles Times*, October 25, 1994, p. 20A.

3. Naomi Wise, "Prospero and Pavarotti," *San Francisco*, October 1982, p. 50.

4. Rebecca Stefoff, *Raul Julia* (New York: Chelsea House Publishers, 1994), p. 58.

5. Personal interview with Lilian Hurst, October 29, 1996.

6. Rick Lyman, "An Actor's Gamble Paid Off Handsomely," *Philadelphia Inquirer*, August 23, 1985, p. 1D.

7. Ibid., p. 6D.

8. Susan King, "'Spider Woman' Part Gives the Kiss of Success to Raul Julia," *Los Angeles Herald Examiner*, August 27, 1985, p. 6C.

9. David Ansen, "An Escape from Escapism," *Newsweek*, August 5, 1985, p. 64.

10. Stephen Hunter, "Raul Julia: Despite Hit, He Faces Actor's Unsure Future," *Baltimore Sun*, September 8, 1985, p. 6G.

11. King, p. 6C.

12. Stefoff, p. 65.

13. Carolyn Beach, "Stardom Beckons Raúl Juliá," *Nuestro*, December 1985, p. 16.

14. Hunter, p. 6G.

15. Lyman, p. 6D.

16. Scott Cain, "Raul Julia Makes Himself Known," *The Atlanta Journal*, January 9, 1986, p. 1P.

17. Jerry Parker, "Raul Julia: An Actor Who Does It All," *Philadelphia Inquirer*, September 8, 1982, p. 5C.

18. Cain, p. 6P.

19. Kathryn Buxton, "A New Beginning for Raul Julia," *Palm Beach Post*, January 4, 1987, p. 13G.

20. Cain, p. 6P.

21. George Hadley-Garcia, *Hispanic Hollywood: The Latins in Motion Pictures* (New York: Carol Publishing Group, 1990), p. 23.

22. Univision TV Network, 1988, as quoted in Hadley-Garcia, p. 13.

23. Personal interview with Lilian Hurst, October 29, 1996.

24. "The Eyes Had It," *People*, November 7, 1994, p. 127.

25. Lawrence Cohn, "Hollywood Full of Busybodies," *Variety*, September 6–12, 1989, p. 4.

26. Tim Johnson, "Actor de Polémico Filme Supervisará Voto Salvadoreño," *El Nuevo Herald*, March 19, 1994, p. 1A.

27. Frank Pérez and Ann Weil, *Raul Julia* (Austin, Texas: Raintree Steck-Vaughn, 1996), p. 34.

28. Stephan Ulstein, "Celluloid Evangelism," *Christianity Today*, November 3, 1989, p. 78.

29. Phoebe Hoban, "Meeting Raul," *New York*, November 25, 1991, p. 56.

30. John Pym, "A Lawyer's Tale," *Sight and Sound*, Autumn 1990, p. 279.

31. David Denby, "Presumed Innocent" (review), *New York*, August 6, 1990, pp. 45–46.

32. Kevin Kelly, "The New Man of La Mancha," *Boston Globe*, March 8, 1992, p. 38B.

33. Hadley-Garcia, p. 223.

34. Anna Quindlan, "Raul Julia—Out of the Ethnic Trap," *The New York Times*, July 10, 1977, p. 5D.

35. Beach, p. 14.

36. Cain, p. 6P.

37. Buxton, p. 13G.

38. Ross Westzsteon, "Raul Julia Is a Sexual Time Bomb," *The Village Voice*, June 14, 1976, p. 141.

39. King, p. 6C.

40. Hoban, p. 54.

41. Paul Hodgins, "Actor Raul Julia's Career Distinguished by Diversity," *The Ottawa Citizen*, October 25, 1994, p. 24.

42. Pérez and Weil, p. 37.

43. Betsy Sharkey, "Making Fresh Ghoulash of the Addamses," *The New York Times*, November 17, 1991, p. 18H.

44. Hoban, p. 54.

45. Sharkey, p. 13H.

46. Kelly, p. 1B.

47. Pérez and Weil, p. 45.

48. Beach, p. 14.

49. Cain, p. 1P.

50. T. E. Kalem, "Pinter-Patter," *Time*, January 21, 1980, p. 84.

51. Robert Brustein, "Journeys to the End of the World," *The New Republic*, February 9, 1980, p. 26.

52. Cain, p. 1P.

53. "The Unofficial Raul Julia Page" (on the Internet at http://www.pratique.fr/~docbrown/).

54. Laurie Winer, "Raul Julia, A Talent Beyond Typecasting," *Los Angeles Times*, October 25, 1994, p. 1F.

55. Alan Rich, "The Burning Season," (review) *Variety*, September 12, 1994, p. 26; John J. O'Connor, "Little Guy as Hero: The Death of Chico Mendes," *The New York Times*, September 16, 1994, p. B4.

56. "The Unofficial Raul Julia Home Page."

57. Personal interview with Kamala López-Dawson.

58. "The Eyes Had It," *People*, November 7, 1994, p. 127.

CHAPTER 7

1. "The Unofficial Raul Julia Page" (on the Internet at http://www.pratique.fr/~docbrown/).

2. Stephen Holden, "Raul Julia's Last Film, with Van Damme," *The New York Times*, December 24, 1994, p. 11.

3. Alberto Minero, "Ultimo Homenaje a Juliá: Puerto Rico Recibirá el Cuerpo de su Hijo," *El Diario/La Prensa*, October 26, 1994, p. 6.

4. Frank Pérez and Ann Weil, *Raul Julia* (Austin, Texas: Raintree Steck-Vaughn, 1996), p. 40.

5. Minero, p. 6.

6. Guy Flatley, "Raul Julia—The Man You Love to Hiss," *The New York Times*, December 26, 1971, p. 5D.

7. Burt A. Folkart, "Raul Julia: Actor Portrayed a Wide Array of Characters on Stage, Screen," *Los Angeles Times*, October 25, 1994, p. 20A.

8. Felix Jerez, "Raúl Juliá: El Mundo Entero Llora su Muerte," *Impacto Latin News*, November 1, 1994, p. 19.

9. Ileana Cidoncha, "Conclusión de los Médicos," *El Nuevo Día*, October 25, 1994, p. 6.

10. Ivan Roman, "Miles en Puerto Rico Rinden Homenaje a Raúl Juliá," *El Nuevo Herald*, October 27, 1994, p. 1A.

11. "Puerto Rico Le Da El Ultimo Adios a Su Hijo Raúl Juliá," *La Prensa*, November 3, 1994, p. 10.

12. Minero, p. 6.

13. Pérez and Weil, p. 38.

14. "Puerto Rico Le Da El Ultimo Adios a Su Hijo Raúl Juliá," p. 10.

15. Eric Pace, "Raul Julia Is Remembered, With All His Panache," *The New York Times*, November 7, 1994, p. 12B.
16. Ibid.
17. Ibid.
18. Roman, p. 1A.
19. *Variety*, October 31, 1994, p. 101.

CHAPTER 8
1. Rebecca Stefoff, *Raul Julia* (New York: Chelsea House Publishers, 1994), p. 91.
2. "Raul Julia," *Performing Artists* (New York: UXL, 1995), p. 360.
3. Allan Wallach, "The Evolution," *Newsday*, October 29, 1978, p. 4.
4. Carolyn Beach, "Stardom Beckons: Raúl Juliá," *Nuestro*, December 1985, p. 12.
5. Phoebe Hoban, "Meeting Raul," *New York*, November 25, 1991, p. 54.
6. Personal interview with Lilian Hurst, October 29, 1996.
7. Andrea Martínez, "Una Estrella en la Vida Real," *El Nuevo Día*, October 25, 1994, p. 5.
8. Susan King, "'Spider Woman' Part Gives the Kiss of Success to Raul Julia," *Los Angeles Herald Examiner*, August 27, 1985, p. 6C.
9. The Hunger Project, "The Raúl Juliá Ending Hunger Fund," March 1995.
10. Tim Johnson, "Actor de Polémico Filme Supervisará Voto Salvadoreño," *El Nuevo Herald*, March 19, 1994, p. 1A.
11. Frank Pérez and Ann Weil, *Raul Julia* (Austin, Texas: Raintree Steck-Vaughn, 1996), p. 43.
12. Lawrence Grobel, "Suddenly, Everybody's *Mad About Helen Hunt*," *Cosmopolitan*, June 1996, p. 157.
13. Stefoff, p. 93.
14. Nancy Rosado Camacho, "Recordando a Raúl Juliá Arcelay" (on the Internet at http://www.pratique.fr/~docbrown/).
15. Personal interview with Lilian Hurst, October 29, 1996.
16. Laurie Winer, "Raul Julia, A Talent Beyond Typecasting," *Los Angeles Times*, October 25, 1994, p. 1F.

17. Stephen Hunter, "Raul Julia: Despite Hit, He Faces Actor's Unsure Future," *Baltimore Sun*, September 8, 1985, p. 6G.

18. Rafael Roncal, "Ha Muerto 'El Hombre de la Mancha,'" *El Pregonero*, November 2, 1994, p. 1; Ivan Roman, "Miles en Puerto Rico Rinden Homenaje a Raúl Juliá," *El Nuevo Herald*, October 27, 1994, p. 1A.

19. Alberto Minero, "En Estado de Coma," *El Diario/La Prensa*, October 21, 1994, p. 3.

20. Kevin Kelly, "The New Man of La Mancha," *Boston Globe*, March 8, 1992, p. 38B.

21. Allan Wallach, "The Evolution," *Newsday*, October 29, 1978, p. 5.

22. Polly Anderson, "Raúl Juliá . . . Se Va Para Siempre en el Esplendor de su Fama," *El Vocero*, October 25, 1994, p. 39.

23. Frank Bruni, "Actor Tried, Mastered Many Roles," *Detroit Free Press*, October 25, 1994, p. 1A.

24. Beach, p. 16.

25. Gigi Anders, "Latin Nights: Raul Julia Among Achievement Honorees," *Washington Post*, September 13, 1995, p. 8B.

26. Guy Flatley, "Raul Julia—The Man You Love to Hiss," *The New York Times*, December 26, 1971, p. 5D.

27. Pérez and Weil, p. 7.

28. Anders, p. 8B.

29. Ibid.

30. Solange Curutchet, "Celebran Inauguración de Fondo de Becas Raúl Juliá," *El Nuevo Herald*, January 31, 1997, p. 4A.

31. Beach, p. 16.

32. "Puerto Rico Le Da El Ultimo Adios a Su Hijo Raúl Juliá," *La Prensa*, November 3, 1994, p. 10.

33. Alberto Minero, "Ultimo Homenaje a Juliá: Puerto Rico Recibirá el Cuerpo de su Hijo," *El Diario/La Prensa*, October 26, 1994, p. 6.

34. Anna Quindlan, "Raul Julia—Out of the Ethnic Trap," *The New York Times*, July 10, 1977, p. 5D.

35. Andrea Martínez, "Una Estrella en la Vida Real," *El Nuevo Día*, October 25, 1994, p. 5.

FURTHER READING

Ellis, Roger, ed. *Multicultural Theatre: Scenes & Monologs from New Hispanic, Asian, & African-American Plays.* Colorado Springs, CO: Meriwether Publishing, Ltd., 1996.

Green, Robina, illus. *Shakespeare's Stories: Histories.* New York: Peter Bedrick Books, Inc., 1988.

Kerins, Tony, illus. *Shakespeare's Stories: Tragedies.* New York: Peter Bedrick Books, Inc., 1988.

Lamb, Charles, and Mary Lamb. *Tales from Shakespeare.* New York: NAL Dutton, 1986.

Michaels, Wendy. *Playbuilding Shakespeare.* New York: Cambridge University Press, 1997.

Pérez, Frank, and Ann Weil. *Raul Julia.* Austin, Texas: Raintree Steck-Vaughn, 1996.

Stefoff, Rebecca. *Raul Julia.* New York: Chelsea House Publishers, 1994.

INDEX